Preface

When the Hotel and Catering Industry Training Board launched its series *An Approach to Systematic Training* almost a decade ago, one of the titles that quickly established itself as an invaluable aid to practising managers, supervisors and trainers in the industry was *Industrial Relations.* Students also found it a useful succinct guide and the book became listed as essential reading on hotel and catering courses from craft level upwards.

In 1981, when the HCITB was planning to publish the fourth edition of *Industrial Relations,* consultation with users of earlier editions established a clear need for a longer, more comprehensive book that would build on the success of its earlier editions by creating an awareness of what can and what needs to be done to foster good employee relations in the hotel and catering industry. Hence the decision to change the title to *Employee Relations.*

This new edition of *Employee Relations* incorporates up-to-date information on current employment legislation, with new sections on statutory sick pay, the first aid regulations, the transfer of an undertaking regulations and changes brought about by the Employment Act 1982. The text of the book has been rearranged into some 21 separate chapters so that the reader can more easily find relevant information.

A publication of this sort clearly cannot take the place of detailed, expert advice and while the HCITB has made every effort to ensure that the information is correct, *Employee Relations* should not be regarded as a complete or authoritative statement of the law. Readers are urged to seek appropriate guidance when they are in any doubt, and will need to note changes in legislation after December 1983. Indeed because there is so much in employee relations that depends on the needs or circumstances of individual employees or organisations, the appendices which are devoted to sources of further information and advice, form a substantial section of this book.

Where the term *he* is used, the provisions apply equally to males and females.

The following abbreviations are used in order to simplify references to legislation:

EA82	Employment Act 1982
EA80	Employment Act 1980
EPA	Employment Protection Act 1975
EP(C)A	Employment Protection (Consolidation) Act 1978
TULRA	Trade Union and Labour Relations Act 1974

The text is clearly signposted throughout:

P	Indicates a matter requiring a clear policy decision or giving practical suggestions to adopt
L	Indicates a legal requirement.

Contents

1 Employee relations in the hotel and catering industry

Firstly, let's define terms. It has been cynically observed that three specialists asked to define 'employee relations' will come up with four differing definitions. There is no universally accepted meaning, though a widely used definition is:

> The practice, or the study of relationships within and between workers, working groups and their organisations and managers, employers and organisations (Marsh *Concise Encyclopaedia of Industrial Relations*).

A simpler definition has been used elsewhere:

> All the issues involved in the reward-work equation.

The reason for the change in title for the fourth edition of this book was that many in the hotel and catering industry seem to have a view of 'industrial relations' as being concerned only with trade unions and employment law. These *are* important in a consideration of the subject, but there is value in taking a wider view of the activity to embrace:

> All the factors in the relationships between employers, staff, and other individuals and institutions involved in the employment process.

Whilst they may disagree on definitions, employee relations specialists are unanimous in saying that to understand any employee relations situation it is necessary to take account of the *institutions and parties* involved and their *ideologies and motives.* The following pages describe these factors in the hotel and catering industry.

2 Institutions and parties

Some of the most significant institutions and parties involved in the hotel and catering industry can be depicted diagrammatically (Figure 1).

Amongst the many external organisations affecting employers and employees are: the British Hotels, Restaurants and Caterers Association (BHRCA), the Brewers' Society, the Confederation of British Industry (CBI), the Advisory, Conciliation and Arbitration Service (ACAS), industrial tribunals, the Central Arbitration Committee (CAC), Employment Appeal Tribunal (EAT), Parliament (via employment legislation), colleges and institutions of further and higher education, and the HCITB.

Figure 1
Institutions
and parties

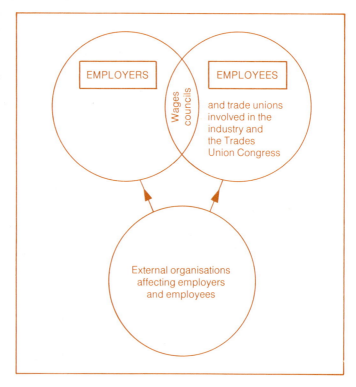

Employers The hotel and catering industry is a heterogeneous industry, consisting of units of many different types often engaged in a multiplicity of activities.

These activities share one or more of three functions: the provision of food, accommodation and/or drink. Hotel and catering is made up of the various types of establishment that provide these commodities and services, usually classified into sectors: hotels, restaurants, the Forces, hospitals, school meals, industrial catering, clubs, pubs, holiday camps, etc.

It is estimated that the industry employs over two million people (full-time, part-time, seasonal, temporary and casual), with approximately 1.6 million in those sectors in-scope to the HCITB and about 500,000 in NHS hospital catering, local authorities and educational catering activities out of scope to the Board.

Each sector of the industry has very different characteristics in terms of activity, size, geographical spread, patterns of ownership and type of workforce. All of these factors have an impact on employee relations.

In recent years there have been many takeovers, so that many operating units are now controlled by large companies. Thus for example, one large organisation now runs a large number of hotels and leisure complexes and has its own industrial catering organisation and airport catering divisions. Other similar organisations operate in the hotel, brewing, industrial catering and popular catering sectors.

Whilst this trend increases the potential for centralised control and standardised procedures, the industry still remains geographically widely scattered and with a relatively small number of staff based at each operating unit (estimated to be 20 on average). These factors are all most important in assessing how to develop good employee relations.

Employers' associations Employers' associations play an important part in negotiating wages and other terms of employment in many industries. At a national level in the commercial sector of our industry there are no employers' associations as such.

The BHRCA, the Brewers' Society and other organisations which are trade associations or marketing consortia, limit their employee relations activities to the provision of advice to their members on staff and personnel matters and to making representation to Government departments, quasi-Governmental agencies, European organisations and other public bodies.

Parliament: employment legislation There is nothing new in Parliament's involvement in employment matters – even in the *laissez-faire* nineteenth century, laws were passed to regulate some aspects of the relationship between employers and employees. More recently, concern over Britain's industrial performance, and over

11

employees' rights led to the passing of a large number of employment laws in the 1970s, a trend which is continuing.

Thus in 1971 the Industrial Relations Act was passed by the Conservative Government in an attempt to regulate and improve industrial relations. It was repealed in 1974 by the Labour Government's Trade Union and Labour Relations Act, but a number of important parts of the 1971 Act – relating to unfair dismissal and to the code of industrial relations practice – were re-enacted by the 1974 Act. The Labour Government then went on to introduce the Employment Protection Act and other legislation.

Taken together, the employment legislation from 1970–78 introduced a large number of individual rights for employees, whilst also attempting to strengthen the position of trade unions (Table 1).

In addition to these provisions, the legislation created or developed bodies to enforce and administer the imple-mentation. The role of industrial tribunals was extended, the

	created or reinforced rights such as	
● Equal Pay Act 1970		● Equal pay for men & women
● Contracts of Employment Act 1972		● Additional remedies in respect of unfair dismissal
● Trade Union and Labour Relations Act 1974		● Time off work for public duties, for trade union duties and activities and training, and to look for new work or to arrange for retraining, if redundant
● Health and Safety at Work, etc, Act 1974		
● Sex Discrimination Act 1975		
● Employment Protection Act 1975		● Guarantee payments
● Race Relations Act 1976		● Insolvency payments
● Trade Union and Labour Relations (Amendment) Act 1976		● Improved minimum period of notice
		● More notice of redundancy
● Employment Protection (Consolidation) Act 1978		● Maternity rights
		● Protection against discrimination on grounds of sex, marriage, race or union activity
		● Safer and healthier working conditions
		● Safety representation
		● Disclosure of information to unions
		● Fuller written terms of employment to be given to employee together with details of disciplinary procedures

Table 1
Summary of rights created or reinforced by employment legislation 1970–78

Central Arbitration Committee (CAC) and Employment Appeal Tribunal (EAT) were established. In addition, the Advisory, Conciliation and Arbitration Service (ACAS) was set up as an extension of the previous existing Conciliation and Arbitration Service.

Much of the legislation behind all this remains in force. However, the Conservative Government which replaced the Labour administration of the '70s has gone on to pass legislation (Employment Acts of 1980 and 1982) with a number of aims:

- to define and more clearly regulate the rights and activities of trade unions and their members
- to assist employers (particularly small employers) by changing some of the unfair dismissal provisions
- to make adjustments to aspects of previous law, such as the administration of guarantee pay
- to deal with other, specific, areas such as the creation of the right to time off work for antenatal care.

It seems likely that employment law will continue to change and develop in the foreseeable future, and with the additional feature that the European Parliament will, increasingly, seek to bring British employment law into line with the rest of Europe.

Industrial tribunals

Set up in 1964 to settle disputes over the payment of levy to training boards, the scope of industrial tribunals has been extended to cover disputes over other matters, including for example, *unfair* dismissal and redundancy and in 1983 they dealt with 39,959 cases. The Central Office of Industrial Tribunals for England and Wales is located in London, and the Central Office of Industrial Tribunals for Scotland is located in Glasgow. There is permanent accommodation for hearing cases at 25 centres in England and Wales and five in Scotland. This is supplemented as necessary by hiring suitable accommodation. On any one day an average of 60 tribunals sit in England and Wales and seven in Scotland.

Cases of alleged discrimination on grounds of sex, marriage, race, colour, nationality or ethnic origins are also dealt with by tribunals, as well as disputes over equal pay and redundancy and a number of other matters. In 1982, over 75 per cent of the applications concerned unfair dismissal; about one-third of these cases were heard by a tribunal, the other two-thirds being settled by agreement between the parties or withdrawn. Of the cases brought to tribunals the applicant was successful on only about 31 per cent of occasions.

Tribunals are important in two ways. They make decisions based on reason and objectivity and can make various awards. Secondly, the case law that has built up as a result of the way in which EAT and to a lesser extent tribunals decide cases, has the effect of helping to define what constitutes good practice in employment matters.

Remedies available to an employee who has won a tribunal case are determined according to the circumstances and the type of case. For example, an employee who has been unfairly dismissed can be awarded:

- reinstatement or re-engagement, if he agrees or
- cash compensation.

The former is preferred by the legislation (your job back, not cash, is the intention), and tribunals are required by law to first consider whether to order reinstatement or re-engagement before they consider awarding compensation. In practice orders for reinstatement or re-engagement are made in only about one per cent of successful applications.

Cash awards are calculated according to a formula:

- basic award, related to age, length of service and pay, current maximum £4,350; plus
- if appropriate, a compensatory award based on cash loss (actual or potential – the employee is expected to have done what he can to mitigate his loss), current maximum £7,500; plus
- award when employer defaults on a re-employment or reinstatement order: 13–26 weeks' pay or 26–52 weeks if sacking was due to race or sex.

The limit on a week's pay for the purpose of calculating awards is revised from time to time. It is currently £145 per week. In theory, a maximum total award of £19,390 can be made but a figure this high is rarely reached. In 1982 about half the awards made were less than £1,201 and less than six per cent of awards were over £5,000.

The Advisory, Conciliation and Arbitration Service

Employers obviously need assistance in understanding and interpreting employment legislation. The Employment Protection Act 1975, Section 1, provided for this in the setting up of the Advisory, Conciliation and Arbitration Service, ACAS, which also has a range of other duties.

ACAS is an independent body corporate not subject to directions of any kind from a Minister of the Crown. It has no legal powers to enforce its recommendations, relying on voluntary acceptance of its work. It is a Treasury-financed body run by a Council consisting of a chairman and nine members – three independent, three TUC-nominated and three CBI-nominated. The regional offices of ACAS are staffed by people with special industrial relations experience.

The title of the organisation, Advisory, Conciliation and Arbitration Service, partly describes its role. It is not generally realised how much advisory work it does, as opposed to the more newsworthy roles of arbitration and conciliation. Overall, it is concerned with the improvement of industrial relations and collective bargaining by:

(a) Providing advice on industrial relations and the development of good personnel practices. This expert advice is free, and available to employers, who should not hesitate to call upon it.

(b) Conciliation in industrial disputes between employers and trade unions.

(c) Conciliation in certain disputes between employers and individual employees (eg unfair dismissal).

(d) Advice on the improvement of collective bargaining procedures.

(e) Production of codes of good industrial relations practice; these codes are of great help and importance in the interpretation of complex and sometimes loosely defined areas of employment legislation.

A code of practice is not legally binding: action in law cannot be taken against an employer solely for non-compliance with a code. Provisions of a relevant code can, however, be taken into account in proceedings before a tribunal. It is likely that tribunals will find that failure by an employer to observe the fundamental recommendations of a code will constitute an unreasonable action.

ACAS codes so far published are on:

(a) *Disciplinary Practice and Procedures in Employment* (reproduced in Appendix V);

(b) *Disclosure of Information to Trade Unions for Collective Bargaining Purposes;*

(c) *Time Off for Trade Union Duties and Activities.*

The Employment Act, 1980, Section 3, provides for the development of further codes on other topics. Such codes (for example, those now available on *Picketing* and the *Closed Shop*) may be issued by the Secretary of State for Employment, if necessary after consultation with ACAS.

The original 1971 *Industrial Relations Code of Practice* still stands (except insofar as it has been replaced by the above codes) and is worth consulting.

Central Arbitration Committee ACAS also works with another body, the Central Arbitration Committee (CAC), which is mainly concerned with arbitration over matters relating to disputes over the disclosure of information to trade unions and time off for trade union duties. Other trade disputes may voluntarily be referred to CAC but few cases have, so far, been dealt with in this way.

Employment Appeal Tribunal This tribunal hears appeals, on points of law, from the industrial tribunals. Except in cases involving exclusion or expulsion from a trade union in a closed shop situation, such appeals cannot be heard on points of fact.

The Employment Appeal Tribunal (EAT) has an important job to carry out in developing consistency in the decisions arrived at by industrial tribunals; the decisions of individual tribunals do not set a precedent (though they may be taken into account by others), whereas EAT decisions do. Because employment legislation is complex, and in some parts loosely defined, different tribunals sometimes interpret it in different ways.

EAT interprets the law in relation to the facts and produces an authoritative judgement which then becomes case law. Industrial tribunals must follow this precedent when dealing with similar facts. There are further possible rights of appeal to the Court of Appeal and the House of Lords on points of law from decisions by EAT.

Wages councils In common with certain other industries in which collective bargaining is not widely developed and where pay tends to be low, much of the hotel and catering industry has its minimum wages and terms of employment set by wages councils. These are bodies set up under the Wages Council Act and consist of equal sides of members representing employers and workers, together with three independent persons unconnected with either side of the industry concerned, one of whom is appointed as chairman. The independent members are appointed by the Secretary of State for Employment but are not responsible to him. The 'side' members are appointed by employers' organisations and trade unions nominated by the Secretary of State.

†The scope provisions of the councils are complex and the relevant wages order should therefore be consulted to determine the actual coverage.

The wages councils† involved in the hotel and catering industry are:

(a) Licensed Non Residential Establishments (LNR) – covering public houses and non residential clubs;

(b) Unlicensed Place of Refreshment (UPR) – covering unlicensed restaurants, cafes and snack bars;

(c) Licensed Residential Establishment and Licensed Restaurant (LRE&LR) – covering licensed hotels and residential clubs (with four or more bedrooms) and licensed restaurants.

There was, until 1976, an Industrial and Staff Canteen Undertakings Wages Council.

Unlicensed hotels and guesthouses, and licensed hotels or guesthouses with fewer than four bedrooms, are not covered by a wages council.

The process of agreeing and producing a new wages council order can be initiated by a proposal from either the workers' or the employers' side. In the example in Table 2 the proposal is made by the workers' side.

When initially set up, over 30 years ago, the catering wages councils were seen as an interim step to regulate terms of employment pending the development of fuller collective bargaining between the parties. If and when it is felt that a wages council is no longer necessary in a particular industry, an application can be made to the Secretary of State for

Table 2
Agreeing and
producing
a new wages
council order

1 Demands for improvements in pay and conditions are voiced and approved by union members at union branch meetings, trade conferences and annual delegate meetings.

2 The claim is then formulated in consultation, where appropriate, with the unions represented on the workers' side of the wages council.

3 The employers' side considers its situation and prepares its case.

4 Carefully prepared statements in support of and against the proposal are presented by each side, generally in advance of the meeting of the wages council.

5 Following the reply from the employers' side the two sides retire to separate rooms to consider their positions. Arguments and counter arguments are made to the chairman, who acts rather like a conciliator. When appropriate, the two sides meet again and settlement may be reached by agreement between the two sides. If the sides cannot agree the rival proposals are carried to a vote of the council where the independent members can give a casting vote. If they vote for the proposal of the workers' side it succeeds; if they support the employers' side the workers' proposal fails and that of the employer succeeds.

6 Notice of Proposal as decided by the council is then circulated to the trade in scope of the council and has to be posted up in every establishment to allow for possible representation by workers, employers or other interested parties within a specified period. Any representations to the published proposal are later considered by the council which can either modify or confirm the original proposal.

7 The order is published by the office of the wages council.

8 A copy of the order must be posted up in every establishment affected in the trade concerned. Its terms become operative from the date fixed by the wages council and must be observed as a minimum by *every employer within scope of the order*.

9 Employers observing less than the minimum terms laid down (whether rates of pay or conditions) can be taken to court and legally forced to comply through prosecution by the wages inspectorate.

Employment for its abolition. A wages council can also be converted into a Statutory Joint Industrial Council (SJIC) which is similar to a wages council, but without the independent members.

In 1980, an application for the conversion to SJIC of the LRE&LR Council was investigated by ACAS but not recommended (see ACAS Report No 18).

At present, the whole future of wages councils is under review. The Government have misgivings about the wages council system and will consider the options on its future when international treaty obligations permit.

The HCITB, colleges and professional associations　Various other organisations play an indirect role in employee relations. The colleges, polytechnics and universities who offer hotel and catering courses, the HCITB, the Hotel, Catering and Institutional Management Association (HCIMA) and other professional and personnel associations are important providers of advice, education and training and increasingly influence the type of employee relations education given to qualified staff entering the industry.

Trade unions   The main aim of a trade union is to represent and advance the interests of its members. In the hotel and catering industry trade union membership levels are generally low in comparison with other sectors of the economy and unevenly spread. Thus in some sectors, such as industrial catering, there are often high levels of union membership amongst the catering staff who frequently belong to the union representing the other employees of the concern. In hotels, the picture varies from, at one extreme, a nationalised hotel group with a closed shop union membership agreement for all staff up to management level, to a large multi-unit leisure and hotel organisation with very low levels of union membership.

The unions mainly involved in the industry are:
- General Municipal Boilermakers' and Allied Trades Union (GMBATU) which has set up a separate organisation to serve the industry, the Hotel and Catering Workers' Union (HCWU)
- Transport and General Workers' Union (TGWU) – particularly active in London hotels and in the leisure and tourism industry
- Union of Shop Distributive and Allied Workers (USDAW) which has members in industrial catering and in restaurants in department stores
- National Association of Licensed House Managers (NALHM), which is said to represent approximately 80 per cent of all pub managers and has a number of union membership agreements
- Transport Salaried Staffs Association (TSSA) and National Union of Railwaymen (NUR) representing staff in ex-British Transport Hotels and in rail catering
- National Union of Public Employees (NUPE).

To avoid inter-union disputes over membership and the waste of resources, an informal 'spheres of influence' agreement exists in some sectors of the industry, whereby the unions active in the industry have agreed the companies with which each union will seek to deal. If inter-union membership disputes should arise, the Trades Union Congress, to which most unions belong, operates a mechanism (the Bridlington Agreement) by which they can be resolved.

The TUC also plays a part by the maintenance of its own Hotels and Catering Committee, which meets regularly to co-ordinate developments and resolve union problems.

Though individual unions differ in their structure, the usual organisation of union structure is shown in Figures 2 and 3.

Locally, union officials from different unions meet regularly at Trade Councils. On a national level, most large independent unions are affiliated to the TUC.

The policy-making body of the unions (Figure 3) is the annual conference, which draws delegates principally from branch and district level.

Figure 2
Trade union
organisation

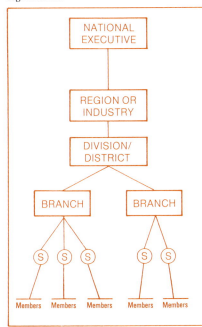

Often full-time and paid; administers the union and provides centralised services – legal, training, research etc; also deals with issues not resolved locally or regionally, responsible to the delegate conference.

At this level union organisation differs between union and industry. District/regional officers are full-time and paid. They deal with the geographical area or activity for which they have been appointed.

Members and staff representatives meet regularly at local branch meetings. Branch officers are unpaid and work part-time.

Staff representatives or shop-stewards, elected by staff, generally unpaid.

Employees who are union members. Each member is assigned to a branch whose meetings he may attend and at which he can vote.

Figure 3
How members
influence union
policy

Members' views are formulated locally and resolutions passed at branch level.

They are then dealt with and, if appropriate, passed on to division/district/region.

If necessary they are debated and can influence and formulate union policy at the delegate conference.

The delegate conference meets generally annually, to consider a report on the year's work and to formulate future policy. Each branch elects at least one delegate to the meeting. Majority decisions of the conference are binding on members, branches, full-time officials, and the union executive.

3 Ideologies and motives

Employee relations is concerned not only with relationships between individuals and institutions, but also with the assumptions and ideas on which these relationships are based.

For example, one commonly held view of employee relations is that the different parties in industry have aims that are in many respects divergent or even conflicting. This 'pluralistic' view holds that such aims, though moderated in practice, mean that the purpose of employee relations has to be to manage and reduce inherent conflict.

On the other hand, an alternative view is that all involved in industry operate as a team, having as their ultimate common goal the success of industry, and that employee relations is about the development of practices to meet this common goal – the so-called 'unitary' approach. Both these sets of extreme views can be firmly and sincerely held; neither can be said to be 'right' or 'wrong'. But individuals with these differing preconceptions will obviously view any given employee relations matter in very different ways.

In raising the question of ideologies and motives, the authors do not wish to make judgements about the validity of these differing views but to make the point that in order to operate effectively, those involved in employee relations (managers, staff and union representatives) need to be aware that:

- peoples' actions are determined partly by their ideals and aspirations
- such ideals vary greatly, and
- we need to understand other peoples' views as well as our own in forming judgements and making decisions†.

In most industries it is accepted that in all but the smallest companies it is useful to have some systematic way of representing employee attitudes and opinions to management – relying on individual contact and consultation is not always possible. This is particularly true when employees' interests clash with those of management – often only some form of third party representation such as is provided by a union, can ensure that justice is seen to be done.

Unions, like employers' associations, have ancillary facilities for research and to help deal with complex matters. Most problems, however, are raised and resolved locally within individual organisations. It is normally better for issues to be handled in this way, between management and union

† For a fuller discussion of this topic, see Fox A, *Industrial Sociology and Industrial Relations,* also Mars, G, *et al, Manpower Problems in the Hotel and Catering Industry* (details on page 113 and the Open University hotels case study (details on page 107)

representatives, where they have been able to build up trust and knowledge of each other and fully understand the problems.

Characteristics of employee relations in the hotel and catering industry

Observers and students of employee relations in the industry have indicated a number of ways in which they feel that the management of employee relations in the hotel and catering industry is affected:

(a) There is much seasonal and part-time work; the demand for the industry's services often being seasonal or erratic and fluctuating.

(b) Many foreign workers, often with a poor command of English, are employed.

(c) Individual hotels, restaurants and canteens are relatively small and widespread, even when belonging to a large organisation, so that control and monitoring of employment practices is difficult.

(d) Relatively few employees belong to trade unions.

(e) A number of trade unions have interests in the industry.

(f) Some employers have reservations about the wisdom of encouraging staff to join unions, feeling that it cannot be beneficial to the unique style necessary for the success of individual enterprises.

(g) The close 'personal' relationship between staff and the customers they serve also affects the management-staff relationship.

(h) There is a preponderance of female employees who have no tradition of trade union membership.

(i) A high incidence of entrepreneurs operate in the industry.

(j) The developments since the early '70s of a professional personnel function in many organisations is having an effect.

(k) There is an absence of employers' associations in the industry.

(l) Labour turnover, which is often extremely high and potentially disruptive, is too readily accepted as normal by many managers and staff.

(m) Often neither staff nor management have experience of formalised systematic employee relations procedures.

It is difficult to evaluate to what extent these general assertions are true, particularly in an industry so large and diverse. There is no doubt, however, that the industry is different from many others in the great potential for job satisfaction that exists in it. Many catering jobs provide satisfying contact with the customer and allow individual flair and creativity. Staff usually have close and frequent contact with their manager or supervisor, unlike the 'anonymous' nature of some factory or office situations. These positive factors should be built on and developed, and in common with other industries there is also:

- an obligation to implement employment legislation
- a need to recognise that long term changes in social attitude are backing up the demands, by staff, for greater involvement in the running of the business
- the increasing cost of labour and other continuing financial and market pressures.

The following chapters suggest some ideas for employment practices that are in line with the current legislation and which should be considered in the light of the points mentioned above.

4 Employee relations policies

One of the continuing main trends of recent employment legislation has been to build on the statutory obligation to clarify the terms and conditions under which staff are employed. Thus, employers are required to provide statements of the main terms of employment and are strongly encouraged to devise and publicise rules and procedures for dealing with discipline and grievance matters.

When an organisation has thought through the way in which it plans to deal with its staff and has communicated this to them, together with a clear statement as to the standards it expects, many potential problems can be avoided.

Checklist 1 contains many of those matters about which it is useful for an employer to have a considered policy.

It is also important that the employer's policies and procedures are known and properly understood by staff and updated as necessary. One or more approaches will assist in this:

1 Effective induction training.

2 Training of those required to implement policy.

3 Use of a staff handbook.

4 Regular consultation and meetings with staff to clarify queries and resolve difficulties.

5 Checking on the effectiveness of communication with members of staff from ethnic minority groups (see *'Qué?'*, HCITB 1981).

In the next chapter employment *practices* are examined in greater depth.

Checklist 1

Developing an employee relations policy

Recruitment
1 What steps have you taken to produce an 'Equal Opportunity' employment policy statement?

2 Do you select on merit – regardless of sex or race?

3 Do you know that the Commission for Racial Equality and the Equal Opportunities Commission can help by giving examples of equal opportunity policies and advice on how to monitor their use? (See Chapter 10.)

Pay and other benefits
4 Do you plan your pay policy?

5 Do you *plan* to be a 'low' or a 'high' payer?

6 Do you know what benefits your competitors offer? (See Chapter 8.)

7 Is your pay structure planned and understood, or based on 'grace and favour'?

8 Do you understand and comply with current wages council orders and with the provisions of the Equal Pay Act?

Staff representation
9 What is your declared approach to staff representation?

10 Do you, where appropriate, recognise and negotiate with a trade union?

11 Do you make adequate facilities available for the representatives of your staff?

12 If you do not recognise a trade union, do your staff have adequate opportunities to represent their views?

Communication and consultation
People are often so busy that (in all but the very smallest organisation) they can easily be unaware of what other working groups are doing or what problems there may be.

13 What do you do to find out about these problems and to help resolve them?

14 How do you consult staff on changes that will affect them and how do you gain commitment to new policies? (See Chapter 14.)

Staff development and training
15 What initiatives have you taken to develop and train your staff, especially young people?

16 Do you have a policy about promotion from within the organisation and do you seek to develop staff by an effective appraisal scheme? (See Chapter 12.)

17 Do you select staff for training and development on the basis of merit and their needs – regardless of sex or race?

Disciplinary matters and grievances

18 Do you have adequate, readily understood procedures that are available for all to see?

19 How are these communicated? (See Chapter 15.)

Retirement

20 At what age do you normally retire staff?

21 How do you decide who is to retire and who can stay?

22 Are your staff aware of the policy and are they clear on whether you have a defined age for retirement?

Redundancy or lay off

23 In what circumstances will staff be made redundant or laid off?

24 What systems of notification, consultation and selection will be used? (Remember that you are obliged to consult the relevant recognised trade union if one exists, and that race and sex discrimination legislation also applies to decisions about redundancy selection.)

25 Are alternatives such as work sharing or short time, built into your procedures? (See page 44 and Chapter 17.)

Finally

Considering your employment policies in general – have they been discussed with your staff?

Even if they do not belong to a trade union, it is preferable to discuss and agree on such matters with staff or their representatives, before making rules.

5 Developing effective employment practices

The hotel and catering industry is an industry of individualists . . . people who like to be independent and to run things with the minimum of outside interference. This approach has much to commend it provided that it is tempered with understanding and a care for the rights of others, especially the staff employed.

Added to this, legislation has given employees considerable rights which it is wrong to ignore and with which employers should be familiar. It is important to realise that employees can no longer be dismissed at will and that in any case labour turnover can be expensive and disruptive. So if in any doubt about a particular topic, don't take a chance – SEEK ADVICE. See Appendix II for sources of help (in particular ACAS).

Most people take the purchase, running and maintenance of specialist equipment and premises as serious matters on which time and money have to be spent. Hiring, employing and dispensing with the services of staff are even more deserving of attention in a labour intensive service industry.

The following chapters give an introduction to sound employment practice. They are necessarily brief, but should assist in deciding whether current employment practices are adequate. Many of those mentioned have been in use by successful employers for some time – they are not theoretical concepts, but well proven techniques.

6 Recruitment and selection

Even in the unemployment-prone 1980s, staff turnover in the hotel and catering industry is high by comparison to other industries. The HCITB's research report *Manpower Changes in the Hotel and Catering Industry,* published in late 1983, confirmed the generally-held belief that staff turnover is highest in the first few months of employment. This is particularly true of the commercial sector where, in hotels and guesthouses, nearly 45 per cent of all new workers left their employer within the first three months (15 per cent in the first month).

Such turnover is costly and emphasises the importance of treating staff recruitment seriously. A manager should decide:

1 Is the job really necessary? Can other jobs be reorganised or reallocated to eliminate this post? Why did the previous employee leave – are there things about the job or supervision that need to be changed? 'Exit' interviews of staff can yield useful information.

2 Is it necessary to recruit outside the organisation? Why not capitalise on the skills already in the organisation by promoting or moving an existing member of staff?

3 What actually is the job? What demands does it make on the person holding it? What personality, qualifications, skill and knowledge will he need to possess? A job analysis – using a simple form – will clarify the demands made by the job and thus the type of person needed to fill it.

4 How should the new staff be recruited? There are many more ways of staff recruitment than putting an advertisement in the newspaper or contacting the local Jobcentre. Different methods and styles should be used and their effectiveness and economy checked. An imaginative approach to recruitment and advertising will attract better quality recruits – important even when staff are easy to come by.

5 Where will the applicants come from? Try to get to know the labour market. Research by NEDO showed, for example, that many hotel managers believed that they had to attract their staff from the existing staff of other hotels and restaurants. In fact, over 50 per cent of hotel staff interviewed in the survey had previously worked *outside* the industry – so the placing of

advertisements (and the subsequent training of new staff) needed to be re-thought. Some London employers have carried out successful local recruitment campaigns in areas well served by direct transport links giving easy access to the business, rather than by general 'blanket' advertising.

6 How should the right person be selected? Carefully!! Most of us think we are good interviewers, just as we believe ourselves to be good car drivers. Possibly neither is correct! In fact, selection interviews are well known to be unreliable and whilst, for a variety of reasons, they will always be widely used, it is necessary to plan interviewing carefully. Checklist 2 sets down a sound approach.

It is also useful to supplement the interview by gaining other information on the candidates from other sources, such as application forms, aptitude and trainability tests. The careful use of references and other techniques can all have an important part to play; training can help develop interviewing skills.

Errors in selection are expensive and difficult to rectify, so it is important to:

1 Be clear about the sort of person being sought.

2 Be knowledgeable about the limitations of interview techniques.

3 Consider the use of other techniques – references, application forms, trainability or selection tests, additional interviews by colleagues – to supplement interviews.

4 Make sure that whatever process of selection is used, it does not discriminate unreasonably against any particular race or sex.

Work permits Foreign, non EEC employees need a valid work permit to work in the UK. The employer needs to apply for this in advance. Permits, issued by the Department of Employment, are issued for a *named overseas worker* and for a *specific job,* and last for no longer than 12 months, though they can be renewed.

Only workers between 23 and 54 years of age are eligible for permits, and the permit will only be issued if no suitable resident labour is available to fill the post concerned. Permits are available for highly skilled and experienced workers to fill senior posts in hotel and catering establishments who have had five years in a skilled capacity, including at least two years in a supervisory position. If the worker has successfully completed an appropriate full-time training course of at least two years' duration at an approved hotel or catering school abroad, this may be allowed to count towards the five years' experience. The Department of Employment leaflet OW5 gives further details.

Checklist 2

Interviewing

Before the interview

1 Draw up a specification of the person sought: experience/ qualifications/education/personality/personal attributes.

2 Plan the interview pattern and timetable.

3 Ensure there will be no interruptions.

4 Brief others involved.

During the interview

5 Put the interviewee at ease.

6 Avoid 'leading questions'.

7 Avoid trick questions.

8 Ask open ended questions.

9 Probe answers if necessary.

10 Don't be afraid of silence.

11 Listen more than you talk.

12 Make notes as necessary.

13 Stick to your timetable.

14 Tell the interviewee when he'll know the decision.

After the interview

15 Make a decision.

16 Take up references.

17 Advise interviewees of results.

18 Keep a record of unsuccessful candidates and reason for rejection.

19 Plan training, especially induction.

20 Check progress after appointment.

Permits may also be issued for 'on-the-job training' or work experience with employers which can be put to use in the trainee's home country but cannot be acquired there. This arrangement is intended to benefit developing countries and their citizens. The training must be for a limited period, as far as possible agreed in advance and extension of approval beyond one year will be given only if satisfactory performance is being maintained.

Before moving from the job for which a permit was issued, the holder must obtain the consent of the Department of Employment.

The Department of Employment leaflet OW22 gives further details.

Sex and race discrimination

It is illegal to discriminate against an applicant on grounds of sex or marriage, except where sex is a *genuine occupational qualification* (see Appendix I), or if five people or fewer are employed†. Remember that the intention of the legislation is to ensure that the applicant selected is the person, of either sex, who is most capable of doing the job.

It is also illegal to discriminate against an applicant on the grounds of race or ethnic origin – except where race is a *genuine occupational qualification* (Race Relations Act 1976).

†In November 1983 the European Court of Justice ruled that the British Government had failed to discharge its obligations under European law by exempting firms with less than six employees, from the Sex Discrimination Act. The Act is thus likely to be amended to include firms of any size.

There are two forms of sex or race discrimination – direct and indirect. *Direct* discrimination occurs when a person is treated less favourably than another, because of sex, race or marital status.

Indirect discrimination consists of applying in any circumstances covered by the Sex Discrimination or Race Relations Acts a requirement or condition which, although applied equally to persons of either sex or all racial groups, is such that a considerably smaller proportion of one sex or a particular racial group can comply with it and that it cannot be shown to be justifiable on grounds other than race or sex.

Allegations of sex or race discrimination in employment matters are dealt with by industrial tribunals. ACAS will attempt conciliation prior to the tribunal hearing. The normal time limit for making a complaint is within three months of the act complained of: a complaint can be made without any qualifying period of employment.

The Equal Opportunities Commission has produced a draft code of practice *For the Elimination of Sex Discrimination and the Promotion of Equality of Opportunity in Employment*. It advocates that all those involved in employment matters (employers, unions, employment agencies) should take certain initiatives to improve the present situation, including:

(a) formulation and circulation of equal opportunities policy statements by employers;

(b) implementing and monitoring such a policy;

(c) examination and improvement of existing recruitment selection and other policies;

(d) greater support from trade unions.

Disabled employees

Firms employing 20 or more staff have a duty to employ a 'quota' of three per cent registered disabled people. In calculating staff numbers, employees working 10–30 hours per week count as one half unit; those over 30 hours as one unit. The Manpower Services Commission is currently considering ways of making the quota scheme more effective within the existing legislation, and is drafting a code of good practice on the employment of disabled people.

The Commission has recently set up a new service for employers, the Disablement Advisory Service, to provide practical advice and guidance on the employment of disabled people, including the specialised help that is available. For example, financial assistance can be given for adaptions to employers' premises, and practical aids to employment can be loaned to disabled employees. The Disablement Advisory Service can be contacted through Jobcentres.

The Rehabilitation of Offenders Act 1974

This Act enables ex-offenders to 'live down' their past and make a new start. The Act specifies that if any offender is not convicted again during a specified 'rehabilitation' period, his conviction becomes 'spent'. The length of the rehabilitation period varies from six months to ten years and only relatively short sentences can be 'spent' in this way.

Under the Act, a spent conviction, or failure to disclose a spent conviction, is not a proper ground for dismissing a person or handicapping him in any way in any occupation or employment. You must not, for example, refer to spent convictions in references you may be asked to provide or you will risk a charge of defamation of character.

Children and young people

There are restrictions on the employment of young people (under 18 years of age) contained in the Shops Act 1950, and the Young Persons (Employment) Act 1938. The former applies to all staff (including kitchen staff) employed in shops or restaurants open to the public and the latter to residential establishments. Section 68 of the Shops Act 1950 allows an employer in a residential hotel, or place of entertainment to give notice to the local authority that all young persons in his employ will be treated as coming under that Act or the Young Persons (Employment) Act, whichever he prefers.

Most hoteliers and caterers may find it convenient to adopt the Catering Trade Scheme (originally in the Shops Act 1913). In general, workers under 18 years of age may not be employed for more than 96 hours per fortnight and may not work more than 50 hours overtime in a year, even if they wish to do so. A minimum of 30 minutes rest must be given in every period of six hours. An important provision covers rests during the night. Young persons must have at least 11 consecutive hours off duty between mid-day and mid-day, including the hours 10 pm to 6 am. There is an exception for boys over 16 years of age employed in serving meals; they are permitted to work until midnight providing they do not start work before 11 am the following day.

Further restrictions on the employment of children are laid down in the Children and Young Persons Act 1933 as amended by the Children and Young Persons Act 1963 and the Children Act 1972. They provide that no child shall be employed:

(a) so long as he is under the age of 13 years; or

(b) before the close of school hours on any day on which he is required to attend school; or

(c) before 7 am or after 7 pm on any day; or

(d) for more than two hours on any day on which he is required to attend school; or

(e) for more than two hours on any Sunday; or

(f) to lift, carry or move anything so heavy as to be likely to cause injury to him.

These restrictions may be made more rigorous by local by-laws. In particular the age below which children are not to be employed can be increased and the employment of children in any specified occupation can be prohibited.

7 Engagement

Having got to the stage where the right staff have been recruited and selected, it is now important to ensure that in the interests of the law, the employer, and the new members of staff, that employees have a simple and clear guide as to the terms and conditions of their employment.

The individual contract of employment is the keystone of the employer-employee relation in law. Once the person who has been selected accepts the job, for the wages offered, the contract is complete. But if there is a dispute later and nothing has been put in writing, it may be difficult to prove the terms of the contract. Mainly because of this the Contracts of Employment Act was first passed in 1963 and now its provisions are covered by the Employment Protection (Consolidation) Act 1978, Section 1.

Written statement

Within 13 weeks of commencing work with an employer, staff working 16 hours a week or more are entitled by law to a *written statement of terms and conditions of employment* (EP(C)A, Section 1).

L

Staff working eight hours or more a week are legally entitled to such a statement only after five years' service, but it is sensible to clarify the situation by providing them with a statement at an early date.

The statutory written statement must contain:

1 Names of employer and employee.

2 Job title (to preserve flexibility it may be useful to add 'and other duties normally associated with this position' to the title).

3 Date of commencement and the date the employee's period of continuous employment began (taking into account whether any employment with a previous employer counts towards that period)

4 Scale of remuneration or method of calculating remuneration.

5 Intervals at which remuneration is paid (monthly, weekly, etc).

6 Any terms and conditions relating to hours of work (including normal working hours).

7 Terms and conditions relating to holidays and holiday pay, incapacity for work due to sickness/injury, sick pay arrangements, pensions and pension schemes (state whether a contracting-out certificate under the Social Security Pensions Act 1975 is in force for the employment in question).

8 Details of disciplinary and grievance procedures and rules, and to whom such matters may be referred (see Chapter 15).

9 Any previous service that counts for continuity purposes and when continuity began.

10 The length of notice which the employee is obliged to give and entitled to receive to terminate his contract of employment (minimum statutory periods of notice have been set, see page 85).

An example of such a written statement is shown in Table 3.

In addition to the above information, which an employer is legally *obliged* to specify, it is important to decide whether to include other matters relating to the business.

Matters commonly giving rise to misunderstanding, and which should therefore be made as clear as possible, include:

1 Conditions under which accommodation or other benefits such as meals or uniform are supplied, and whether accommodation must be vacated when employment ceases.

2 Terms of joint (husband and wife) contracts.

3 Company right to search employees.

4 Deductions from wages.

5 Right to suspend employees and whether this is to be with or without pay (see Appendix V, para 12c).

6 Responsibility as to safety.

7 Continuity of employment (especially for seasonal or casual staff).

8 Maternity rights (see Chapter 9).

9 Requirement to undertake overtime working.

It is important to *check* whether staff understand what they have been told about the rules and procedures, especially if foreign staff are employed who may have language difficulties. In particular, check that they understand:
- whom they should approach to resolve problems
- disciplinary rules
- grievance procedure
- safety/fire/hygiene rules.

Table 3
Written
statements
required by the
Employment
Protection
(Consolidation)
Act 1978.

Introduction

Part I of this statement sets out particulars of the terms and conditions on which I . . . (*name of employer*) . . . am employing you . . . (*name of employee*) . . . at . . . (*date on which statement is issued*).

Part II of this statement sets out information on disciplinary rules, whom you should contact if you wish to appeal against a disciplinary decision or to take up a grievance, and the subsequent steps to be followed in the disciplinary and grievance procedures.

Your employment with me began on . . . (*date*). Your previous employment with…(*name of previous employer or employers*)… counts as part of your continuous period of employment which therefore began on . . . (*date continuous period of employment commenced*) . . .

Alternatively
Your employment with me began on . . . (*date*). Your employment with your previous employer does not count as part of your continuous period of employment.

PART I

1 You are employed as a . . . (*insert job title*).

2 Scale or rate of remuneration, or method of calculating remuneration and the intervals at which remuneration is to be paid . . . (*give details*).

3 Normal hours of work and any other terms and conditions relating to hours of work . . . (*give details*).

4 Holidays and holiday pay . . . (*give details*).

5 Terms and conditions relating to incapacity for work due to sickness or injury and sick pay (*if none, say so*) . . . (*give details*).

6 Pensions and pension schemes (*if none, say so*) . . . (*give details*) . . . (*also state whether a contracting-out certificate under the Social Security Pensions Act 1975 is in force*).

7 Amount of notice of termination to be given by:
(a) The employee . . . (*give details*).
(b) The employer . . . (*give details*).

(*If the contract is for a fixed term no period of notice should be given but the date on which the fixed term expires should be stated.*)

This example
shows a
possible format,
which should be
changed or
amplified as
necessary.

PART II

1 The disciplinary rules which apply to you in your employment are . . . (*explain them*).

35

Table 3 continued

Alternatively

1 The disciplinary rules which apply to you in your employment can be found in . . . (*here reference should be made to a handbook or other document which is given to the employee with the written statement and additional note, or, if that is not practicable, can be read by the employee in a place to which he can gain access without difficulty*).

2 If you are dissatisfied with any disciplinary decision which affects you, you should appeal in the first instance to . . . (*give the name of the person to whom the appeal should be made, or the position which he holds, for example, supervisor*).

3 You should make your appeal by . . . (*explain how appeal should be made*).

Alternatively

3 The way in which appeals should be made is explained in . . . (*refer to an accompanying handbook or a document which is reasonably accessible to the employee*).

4 If you have a grievance about your employment you should apply in the first instance to . . . (*give the name of the person with whom your grievance should be raised or the position which he holds, for example, personnel officer*).

5 You should explain your grievance by . . . (*explain how grievances are to be raised*).

Alternatively

5 The way in which grievances should be raised is explained in . . . (*refer again to an accompanying handbook or, if necessary, to a document which the employee can consult which is reasonably accessible to him*).

6 Subsequent steps in the firm's disciplinary and grievance procedures are . . . (*explain them*).

Alternatively

6 Details of the firm's disciplinary and grievance procedures are set out in . . . (*refer to an accompanying handbook or, if necessary, another document which is reasonably accessible to the employee*).

Note that the separate stages outlined in Part II can be telescoped where, for example, the same person is the first to be approached for appeals against disciplinary decisions and grievances, or where the method of application for both is the same.

Keeping the written statement up-to-date

If there is a change in any terms of employment the employer must *inform* the employee about it, no more than one month after its introduction, by means of a further written statement. He may use other documents (pension booklets, rule books etc) as reference sources to back up the written statement. If these documents are amended, he does not have to send a further written statement, so long as, in the original written statement referring to the documents, he undertakes to keep them up-to-date (within one month of each change).

Do not forget that, once agreed, the terms of a contract of employment should not be changed without the consent of both parties. Some contracts have a built-in degree of flexibility (eg mobility clauses or pay rates based on national agreements). In general, however, if it is necessary to make a change in the terms of an employment contract, it is sensible to consult and agree the change with staff beforehand, rather than attempt to impose a change unilaterally, thus risking a claim for constructive dismissal.

When issuing a statement of terms and conditions of employment, employers can ask an employee to sign to acknowledge receipt of the document, and this is a useful practice, avoiding possible disputes about whether information about a particular matter was or was not given at the start of employment. The employee does not *have* to sign; in such an event a record should be kept that the document was given to him.

Finally, note that if there is a change of employer in a business, staff must be issued with a new and full written statement within 13 weeks of a change. However, if the identity of the employer is unchanged but the name is changed, or if continuity of employment (see Appendix I) is otherwise preserved, the employer need only notify his employees, in writing, within a month, of the change of identity or new name, specifying the date on which the employee's continuous term of employment began. (See also Chapter 18, *Employment rights on the transfer of an undertaking.*)

Part-time and seasonal staff

The hotel and catering industry employs many part-time and seasonal staff. In the past, many of the provisions of employment legislation did not apply to them but the situation has now changed. Staff contracted to work 16 hours or more a week, or eight hours a week after five years with an employer, are entitled to most of the protection and benefits (notice, ability to claim unfair dismissal after a period of employment etc) once given only to full-time staff.

It is good practice to provide terms of employment, benefits, facilities, and services to part-time and casual staff on a pro-rata basis to full-time employees.

At the time of writing the EEC is formulating a Community Directive on part-time workers. It is proposed that they be guaranteed the same rights as full-time employees and discrimination against them be removed. Thus it is likely that part-time employees will have rights to be included in social security schemes, and will be entitled to pay, holiday pay, redundancy pay and retirement benefits on a basis proportional to the hours they work in relation to a full-time employee.

There is obviously a possibility that confusion may arise if staff are taken on as casuals or temporaries and subsequently, because of work needs, become full-time. Does their casual or part-time employment count towards establishing continuity? Particular difficulties can occur with permanent casuals who, in theory are taken on separately for each day's employment but may ultimately claim that de facto continuity of employment has built up.

The key case on this topic, at the time of writing, is *O'Kelly and others v THF* Court of Appeal, 20.7.83. It gives little concrete guidance but clearly raises the issues in question.

The matters looked at by EAT and Court of Appeal in significant 'casual worker' cases are:

- provision and maintenance of equipment/uniform
- method and rate of payment
- hours of work
- extent to which there is a settled relationship between employer and worker
  - similarity in nature of work to full-time employees
  - methods of arranging PAYE, NI payments, and training
  - other contract terms (holidays/sick pay/pensions etc).

Particular attention has been paid to the express intention defined in the contract or 'statement of terms', to custom and practice, and to the extent to which the worker has a 'duty to work' (and for the employer a duty to provide work).

The key to avoiding trouble lies in proper discussion at the time of engagement or when conditions are changed, backed up by adequate documentation.

If in doubt, employers should consult a solicitor, ACAS, their trade association, or one of the other sources listed in Appendix II for help in drawing up the necessary standard letters.

Temporary staff

EEC legislation is being drafted (at the time of writing) to ensure that whilst legitimate temporary work should not be discouraged, those engaged on such work, or with fixed duration contracts should enjoy the same social and other conditions that apply to the permanent workforce.

Other points about contracts

A contract of employment exists between an employer and employee once the latter has accepted an offer of employment from the employer; the fact that, at this stage, the contract is unwritten does not alter the fact that it exists, though it does make it more difficult to resolve disputes that may arise.

In addition, whatever the 'written statement' says, employers and employees have certain duties to one another, under Common Law.

An *employee* must:
- obey all lawful and reasonable orders
- not commit misconduct
- give faithful and honest service
- use reasonable skill and care in his work.

An *employer* must:
- take reasonable care for the employee's safety
- pay the agreed wages
- not require the employee to do unlawful acts
- provide work for workers paid by results or commission if work is available.

Helping new staff settle in

Labour turnover is high throughout the industry. It occurs especially within the first few weeks or months of employment. A report published in 1969 by the Hotel and Catering Economic Development Committee, *Staff Turnover,* disclosed that throughout the industry as a whole, about 70 per cent of all newcomers to the industry left their employment within the first few weeks or months.

The costs of recruiting and engaging a new member of staff are considerable – not only the direct costs like advertising, agency fees, paper-work, interview time, but the many hidden or indirect costs. For example the expenses incurred in training and supervising new entrants, as well as those they are replacing, overtime that may have been paid during staff shortages, an increase in wastage and losses while new staff settle in, customer irritation and low staff morale if staff turnover is high.

Thus the first few weeks of employment are a vital period in the long term retention of staff. An effective induction programme will help new staff settle into their new job as soon as possible, by familiarising them with:
- the job and its surroundings
- the people they will be working with
- essential information about the industry, the employer and their conditions of employment.

Table 4 gives further details.

Employee Relations

Table 4
When and how
induction can
take place

When

Induction begins from the first contact any prospective new employee has with your organisation – first impressions are important. The main stages are:

when staff are being interviewed and appointed;
the day they start;
during and after the first few weeks.

How
Before joining by:

dealing courteously and efficiently with applicants for jobs

saying something about the company

explaining the type of work

showing recruits where they will be working

giving them details of conditions of work

introducing them to the person to whom they will be directly reporting

ensuring that they know where and when they start

giving them, where available, an employee handbook.

On the first day by:

welcoming and introducing

showing around

checking explanations already given about conditions of work

explaining main features of job standards, health and safety requirements, necessary procedures, etc

introducing to someone who can answer queries, show the ropes, etc

introducing to workers' representatives

going over employee handbook

explaining training.

During the first few weeks, by:

arranging attendance at a short induction course

using a checklist to see that further information and introduction are given as employee settles in

encouraging newcomers to find out some things for themselves

maintaining regular interest in how they are getting on

arranging follow-up interview with manager.

You will notice that much of this can only take place on the job, involving managers, supervisors and colleagues.

8 Pay policies and procedures

Labour is one of the major costs in the industry and one of the few variables that can be controlled over a short term period. It is not easy to reduce the size of a restaurant, but it is normally possible to improve the productivity of the staff.

Furthermore, the industry has a 'low pay' image; if this is to be overcome and therefore better quality staff attracted, it is important that staff are clear about the value of the pay and other benefits in kind they receive, for example meals and accommodation.

A well thought out pay policy is thus important, and with this in mind, Checklist 3 offers a number of fundamental questions employers might find it useful to consider.

Checklist 3

Developing a pay policy

1 Is it appropriate to the size and type of establishment, and the calibre of staff employed?

Paying the statutory minimum may only allow the recruitment of low grade staff. Paying higher rates may enable an employer to operate with fewer staff, providing good service at the same total cost.

2 How are wage levels fixed?

Wages surveys can give accurate information on what other employers in the industry are paying, as well as what other employers may be offering *your* staff to attract them to another industry.

3 How are pay differentials decided?

Job evaluation techniques are especially useful in larger organisations where it can otherwise be difficult to establish fair differentials between groups of staff. Pay grievances often stem from staff who are dissatisfied with their earnings in comparison with others, and job evaluation is a fair and more acceptable way of establishing differentials. ACAS can provide assistance in job evaluation, and have produced a free publication: Advisory Booklet No 1 *Job Evaluation*. The Industrial Society can also assist.

4   Does the pay system aim to reward effort by some form of bonus, or are other incentives such as profit sharing or merit rating used?

They may be worth considering; if such a system already exists, remember to check that it is still operating effectively.

5   Is it clear to staff exactly what 'perks' or fringe benefits they are entitled to?

The industry has its fair share of dishonesty: 'fiddles' over money or goods and such practices do not bring about good relations with staff. Many employers have found that clarifying these matters has been helpful to them. (Some writers on employee relations in the industry feel strongly that it is inappropriate to attempt to deal with such matters purely by the establishment of procedures and policies. They advocate taking account of many other factors such as the cultural values of the staff and their particular relationship with management and with the customer. For a fuller discussion, see the book by Gerald Mars *et al, Manpower Problems in the Hotel and Catering Industry.*)

6   Do staff really understand the wages and benefits they will receive?

7   Can the pay structure be simplified?

Misunderstanding breeds suspicion and lack of trust. Many organisations have complicated or unorthodox pay schemes that can cause confusion. Matters reported as often causing difficulty in our industry include:

● payment of a fixed cash sum 'in the hand'
● shift arrangements and pay rates
● distribution of tips or service charge.

Further information on different payment schemes will be found in ACAS Advisory Booklet No 2 *An Introduction to Payment Systems.*

Minimum wage

As explained in Chapter 2, wages councils determine the minimum wages and terms of employment for many sectors of the hotel and catering industry.

The Employment Protection Act extended the powers of wages councils. They can now fix any terms and conditions of employment and are no longer restricted to those affecting pay and holidays. They can also fix dates from which new pay and terms of employment shall operate.

Various press and other reports, and investigations by the wages council inspectorate, have drawn attention to the fact that some employers contravene wages council requirements by failing to display information on minimum rates of pay, or by paying below those rates. Employers who break the law in this way can be fined and required to pay arrears.

The provision of the Employment Protection Act (Schedule 11) that employers covered by a wages council could not pay less than the lowest rate negotiated by a union in that industry through voluntary collective bargaining with an employers' association or employers at a significant number of establishments in a district or the industry, was abolished by the Employment Act 1980.

The Fair Wages Resolution which provided that Government contracts would not be awarded to those paying less than the recognised, or comparable 'rate for the job', has also now been abolished.

The Truck Acts

The principal objective of the Truck Act 1831 was to stop payment of wages in kind. It enacted that certain classes of workmen were to be paid in coin of the realm and not otherwise, that contracts providing for payment of wages otherwise than in coin were void, that an employer could not impose conditions on the manner in which or the person with whom the wages were spent and that if the employer sold goods to the workman on credit he could not recover the price of them from the workman.

The Truck Amendment Act 1887 extended the classes of persons protected by the 1831 Act. It defined 'workman' as a person engaged in manual labour under a contract of service with an employer.

The Truck Act 1896 was passed in order to put on a proper footing the question of deductions for fines, damaged goods and materials or services supplied by the employer. Even where the Act permits deductions these are subject to the satisfaction of certain conditions. For example, the contract of employment must state the acts or omissions for which a deduction can be made and any deduction must be fair and reasonable.

Payment of Wages Act 1960

The Payment of Wages Act 1960 allows workers to opt at their written request to have wages paid into a bank account. Either the employer or the worker can cancel the arrangement provided four weeks' notice in writing is given. The Government has stated its intention to accelerate the trend toward cashless pay by repealing the Truck Acts whilst retaining protection for employees against arbitrary deductions from wages.

Itemised pay statement

Under the Employment Protection (Consolidation) Act 1978, employers must issue an itemised pay statement to all employees who normally work 16 hours a week or more (or eight hours if they have five or more years' service). The statement must contain:

(a) Gross wages or salary.

(b) Amounts of any fixed deductions and the purposes for which they are made (eg contributions to National Savings

Employee Relations

Schemes authorised by the employee to be deducted from his pay). It is permissible for the employer to show only the aggregate amount provided he has already given the employee a standing statement of fixed deductions. This statement must be renewed annually.

(c) Amounts of any variable deductions and the purposes for which they are made (eg income tax, national insurance).

(d) Net wages or salary.

(e) Where different amounts of the net wage or salary are paid in different ways, the amount and method of payment of each part payment (eg wages paid weekly, distribution of bonus monthly).

The intention behind this requirement is that employees will understand how their pay is made up, and the purposes for which deductions are being made.

A Court may make an Attachment of Earnings Order, instructing an employer to make a deduction from the earnings of an employee who has defaulted on payment of a debt, fine or maintenance.

For further information see the HMSO publication *The Attachment of Earnings Act 1971, Explanatory Booklet for Employers.*

Guarantee payments

The Employment Protection (Consolidation) Act 1978, as amended by the Employment Acts 1980 and 1982, states that an employee who works 16 hours a week or more, or 8–16 hours a week and has been continuously employed for at least five years is entitled to a guarantee payment if he loses pay because of short-time working or lay offs,† provided:

(a) A full day's work is lost.

(b) The employee has completed one month's service.

(c) The employee has not unreasonably refused an offer of suitable alternative work.

(d) The short time or lay off does not result from a trade dispute involving any employee of the employer or an associated employer.

† The Act does not give employers the right to lay off staff. There is no such statutory right and the terms and conditions of an individual's contract of employment, whether written or not, must provide for such a circumstance.

Guarantee payments are limited to one day's pay (subject to a ceiling figure, at present (1984) £10 up to a maximum period of five workless days in any three month period, or the equivalent number of days per week normally worked by that employee).

Temporary employees taken on to work for up to three months are not eligible for guarantee payments.

Wages council orders contain overriding provisions for guaranteed pay. The appropriate orders should be referred to for current requirements.

Further information is available in the Employment Legislation booklets, No 9 *Guarantee Payments* and No 11 *Rules Governing Continuous Employment and a Week's Pay* (DE).

44

Insolvency

Under the insolvency provisions of the Employment Protection (Consolidation) Act 1978, the Department of Employment may pay from the Redundancy Fund certain debts owed to employees by insolvent employers. These include arrears of pay (for one or more weeks up to a maximum of eight weeks), holiday pay (up to a maximum of six weeks) and a compensatory payment for the employer's failure to give the employee proper statutory notice. A financial limit is imposed on each debt (currently £145 a week, this amount is revised from time to time). Further information is available in the No 3 booklet in the Employment Legislation series *Employee's Rights on Insolvency of Employer.*

Time off work

The Employment Protection (Consolidation) Act entitles employees to reasonable time off work under certain circumstances (pregnant employees are also allowed time off with pay for antenatal care, see Chapter 9):

With pay

● for officials of independent, recognised trade unions to carry out official duties connected with industrial relations between the employer (and any associated employer) and the employees; and for TUC or union-approved industrial relations training (see ACAS Code of Practice No 3) (EP(C)A Section 27)

● an employee who is being made redundant is entitled to reasonable time off to look for work or to arrange training for a new job provided he has been continuously employed for at least two years (EP(C)A Section 31).

● for safety representatives (appointed by recognised trade unions) to perform their duties and undergo TUC-approved training. For further information see the Health and Safety Commission's booklet *Safety Representatives and Safety Committees.*

Without pay†

†That is employees have a right to receive unpaid time off for these purposes, an employer may of course pay them if he wishes.

● for members of an independent recognised trade union to take part in that union's activities (other than industrial action) (EP(C)A Section 28)

● for public duties, employees who are JPs or are members of certain public bodies (see Table 5) are entitled to reasonable time off to carry out necessary duties subject to the needs of the business (EP(C)A Section 29).

The ACAS Code of Practice No 3 gives more details on time off for trade union duties and activities.

Table 5
Time off for
public duties

> An employer shall permit an employee of his who is:
>
> a JP
>
> a member of a local authority
>
> a member of any statutory tribunal
>
> a member of a Regional or District Health Authority (England and Wales) or Health Board (Scotland)
>
> a member of – in England and Wales – the managing or governing body of an educational establishment maintained by a local educational authority, or in Scotland, a school or college council or the governing body of a central institution or a college of education
>
> a member of a water authority (England and Wales) or River Purification Board (Scotland)
>
> to take reasonable time off during working hours to perform the duties of his office or as a member.

Medical suspension

Section 19 of the Employment Protection (Consolidation) Act provides for an employee with one month's service or more, who has to be suspended from work under statutory regulations following examination by a member of the Employment Medical Advisory Service or an appointed doctor, to be entitled to be paid normal wages for the time of suspension up to a maximum of 26 weeks. This payment applies in certain situations where it would be injurious *to the health of the worker* for him to continue to work. The situations are clearly laid down in Schedule 1 to the Act as amended and include lead smelting, radioactive substances etc.

There has been little impact on our industry as a result of this provision though both the Secretary of State for Employment and the Health and Safety Commission are empowered to extend the coverage by regulations or codes of practice.

Holiday pay

In Britain there is no general statutory right to any paid holiday. Minimum conditions are, however, set for the relevant parts of the hotel and catering industry by the wages councils concerned. There has been a general trend towards longer holidays, together with pressure to reduce the length of the working week.

If staff request extended leave to visit friends or relatives overseas, make sure that the terms of such leave (how long, notification of delays, length of time a job is to be kept open) are clearly agreed, understood and preferably put in writing before the leave starts. The fact that you have done so does not automatically mean that it is fair to dismiss an employee who does not return on time, but it will be helpful in justifying your subsequent action.

Maternity pay This is dealt with in the next chapter.

Pensions Considerable attention is nowadays being paid to pensions as a form of 'deferred income'. The Social Security Pensions Act 1975 was aimed at improving pension benefits. Employers who operate their own pension schemes need to check whether they meet the minimum criteria imposed by the Government, and to indicate the position in writing to their staff (this is usually done in the written statement of terms and conditions of employment).

The subject is a complex one. Further guidance may be obtained from the Department of Health and Social Security and from pension specialists.

Sick pay The Social Security and Housing Benefits Act 1982 created the right for all employees, subject to certain exclusions, to receive statutory sick pay (SSP).

This is paid to employees by their employer, who recovers the payments he has made from national insurance contributions.

SSP does not relieve an employer from making any other sickness payments that may be given as part of a contractual obligation, though it can be counted as contributing towards them.

SSP is payable for the first eight weeks of sickness and is based on the level of an employee's average earnings over the previous eight weeks.

SSP amounts are adjusted by the Government from time to time: at the time of writing the maximum weekly rate, for an employee with average weekly earnings of over £65, is £40.25.

Employees are excluded from receiving SSP if they are:

(a) over pensionable age;

(b) on short term contracts (those of less than three months, provided that this period is specified in the contract at the outset; if not so specified, the employee will be entitled to SSP);

(c) average earnings are below the national insurance threshold (at the time of writing) £32.50 per week;

(d) who have already received certain social security benefits such as invalidity benefit;

(e) who have not yet started work with the employer;

(f) are sick during a stoppage of work involving a trade dispute at their place of employment, unless they have not taken part and have no direct interest in it;

(g) who have already exhausted their entitlement;

(h) who are pregnant and fall sick within the 'disqualifying period' (the period of 18 weeks beginning with the eleventh week before the expected week of confinement);

(i) are in prison or in legal custody;

(j) fall sick abroad in a non EEC country.

The method of calculating entitlement to SSP involves defining four terms:

Period of incapacity for work

A *period of incapacity for work* (PIW) is any period of four or more consecutive days, each of which is a day of incapacity for work. Any two PIW's which are separated by a period of not more than two weeks shall be treated as a single PIW (known as 'linking'). Any day is included in calculating a period of consecutive days, even if it was a rest day.

Qualifying days

These are the days of the week on which an employee is required by his contract of service to be available for work, or which are chosen to reflect the terms of that contract.

Waiting days

These are the first three qualifying days in any period of entitlement. No SSP is paid for waiting days.

Period of entitlement

This is the period, to a maximum of eight weeks in any one tax year, for which SSP is paid. Entitlement also ends when an employee's PIW, or series of linked PIW's, spanning two tax years reach eight weeks.

In addition, the period of entitlement ends if:
- an employee is no longer incapable for work
- an employee reaches the eleventh week before the one in which her baby is due
- an employee's contract of service comes to an end
- an employee goes abroad outside the EEC
- an employee is taken into legal custody.

The DHSS will want to know two weeks before an employee's period of entitlement is ending if his PIW is expected to continue. Form SSP1(T) is completed by the employer and given to the employee to enable him to claim State sickness benefit.

SSP has involved a change in the procedure for obtaining a doctor's certificate. Doctor's certificates are now not available for periods of absence of less than eight days. An employee must produce reasonable evidence to his employer to support a claim for SSP. A DHSS form (SC1) is available, but many employers prefer to produce their own form which can also be used for any other absences that have not been approved in advance.

Rules are necessary to guide employees in such arrangements as when to apply, and how to notify absence through sickness.

Doctor's certificates are still provided for absences of more than eight days.

In order to administer sick pay schemes effectively, employers will require efficient staff records (see Chapter 11) detailing such information as:

- dates of sick absence reported by employee
- dates SSP not paid – with reasons
- details of agreed week (qualifying days)
- date doctor's statement received, and a copy of it
- days for which SSP was paid, and the amounts.

A number of commercial organisations have produced comprehensive administrative systems – some computerised – to assist in the task. Make sure that if you are responsible for sick pay, you also use the system to monitor absenteeism and reduce it to the minimum: it is a costly problem to many organisations.

Tax deduction sheets include a column for recovering SSP. The employer enters amounts paid on the employee's cards and on his monthly return. The gross amount of SSP paid to employees is deducted from the national insurance payments that the employer is due to make.

Equal pay and sex discrimination

The Equal Pay Act 1970 (which came into force on December 29, 1975) as amended by the Equal Pay (Amendment) Regulations 1983 and the Sex Discrimination Act 1975 prevent employers from discriminating between men and women, whether adults or juveniles, in pay, recruitment, conditions of employment, or in the way they treat employees in such matters as promotion, transfer, training, benefits or dismissal.

The Equal Pay Act has the effect of writing an equality clause into a woman's contract of employment and is designed to eliminate sex discrimination from the areas of pay and conditions of employment. The Act applies to all employees regardless of the size of the firm for which they work, how long they have been employed or how many hours per week they work. Since December 29, 1975, the Equal Pay Act has given a woman the right to equal pay and other contractual terms of employment when she is doing the same or broadly similar work or work rated as equivalent under a job evaluation scheme as a man employed by the same or an associated employer, unless the employer can show that there is a material difference, other than the difference of sex, between the woman's case and the man's. Since January 1, 1984, the Act has also given a woman (and a man) the right to equal pay and other contractual terms of employment when she is doing work of equal value as a man employed by the same or an associated employer.

Individuals who feel that they are entitled to equal pay can take a claim to an industrial tribunal whilst they are employed or at any time up to six months after they have left the employment concerned.

If collective agreements or pay structures contain provisions relating specifically to men or women only they can be referred to the Central Arbitration Committee for amendment.

The Sex Discrimination Act requires employers not to discriminate between men and women, for example:

- not to treat a person of one sex less favourably than a person of the opposite sex, on the grounds of their sex
- not to apply a condition or requirement to both sexes if this has the effect of excluding considerably more persons of one sex and cannot be justified
- not to treat a married person less favourably than an unmarried person of the same sex because that person is married
- not to apply a condition or requirement which has the effect of discriminating against married people because considerably fewer married than single people of the same sex can comply with it, and which cannot be justified
- not to treat a person less favourably than another person of either sex in the same circumstances because that person has taken, or is suspected of taking, action or helping another person to take action, under the Sex Discrimination Act or Equal Pay Act (these provisions do not apply if the person has made allegations which are false and are not made in good faith).

There are exceptions in which discrimination (but not victimisation) may be lawful, principally they are:

(a) Where not more than five people are employed†. Part-time employees count as full employees, and employees of associated employers are included.

(b) Employment in a private household.

(c) Where a genuine occupational qualification (GOQ) exists, for considerations of decency or privacy, or where the job holder has to live in premises which are normally lived in by people of one sex, which do not have private sleeping or sanitary facilities which could be used by a person of the opposite sex, and where the employer could not reasonably be expected to provide alternative facilities for the opposite sex, or the job is one of two held by a married couple. Note that the Act states specifically that where strength or stamina are required for a job, sex is *not* a GOQ.

In order to avoid allegations of sex discrimination it is necessary to be particularly careful when advertising vacancies to avoid job titles like 'waiter' or 'chambermaid' without indicating that applicants of either sex will be considered, and to avoid using expressions in the body of the advertisement that indicates a preference for either sex, for example 'attractive blonde'. An illustration depicting a man or woman in the role could be open to a charge of discrimination.

†In November 1983 the European Court of Justice ruled that the British Government had failed to discharge its obligations under European law by exempting firms with less than six employees from the Sex Discrimination Act. The Act is thus likely to be amended to include firms of any size.

9 Maternity provisions

Some of the provisions of the Employment Protection (Consolidation) Act 1978 relating to maternity have been changed by the Employment Act 1980. The situation is as follows.

Antenatal care

The Employment Act provides pregnant employees with the right not to be unreasonably refused to paid time off to attend for antenatal care on the advice of a doctor, midwife or health visitor. *There is no qualifying period of employment.*

The woman may be asked to produce, for the inspection of her employer, proof of her appointment for antenatal care (except for the first appointment) and a certificate of pregnancy. If she does this, and is unreasonably refused permission to attend, she can complain to an industrial tribunal, who can order the employer to pay her the sum she would have received had she been given the time off (based on the appropriate hourly rate).

Right to return to work

The law gives an employee who leaves work to have a baby the right to return to her job at any time before the end of 29 weeks beginning with the week in which the baby is born subject to the following conditions:

(a) An employer with five or fewer workers (including those employed by any associated employer) is exempt from the obligation to allow a woman to return to work if he can demonstrate that it is not 'reasonably practicable' for him to do so, or he cannot offer suitable alternative work.

(b) Employers are not necessarily required to reinstate women in their original jobs – they may offer a 'suitable alternative' job, so long as the terms and conditions are not 'substantially less favourable' than those of the original job.

An employee may postpone her return to work for up to an extra four weeks if she is unfit for work, so long as she can produce a medical certificate to this effect, and an employer also has the right to postpone her return up to four weeks so long as he gives her a reason for doing so.

In order to qualify for the right to return, a woman must: continue to be employed up to 11 weeks before the expected time of confinement (that is her contract of employment must still exist, even though she may not be working, because for example, she is on leave); and at that time have at least two years' service (or five years' service if she works less than 16 but more than eight hours per week). Also:

(a) She must inform the employer that she will be absent from work due to pregnancy or confinement, that she intends to return to work with him and notify him of the expected date of confinement. She must do so in writing at least 21 days before her absence begins; if it is not reasonably practicable to do so by that date, she must inform him as soon as it is reasonably practicable.

(b) Not less than 49 days after the beginning of the expected date of confinement, if the employer requests written confirmation that she intends to return to work, she must provide such confirmation within 14 days, or she will not be entitled to the 'right to return'.

(c) At least three weeks before intending to exercise her right to return to work, she must notify her employer, in writing, of her intention to return – or lose the right.

This is a complex system, and to avoid misunderstanding and difficulties, employers should make sure that their records and administrative systems are efficient and well understood, and that pregnant employees are clear about their rights and obligations.

Now that the minimum period of employment qualifying an employee to claim for unfair dismissal has been raised to one year, the taking on of replacements to 'cover' for women on maternity leave presents less difficulty, since the replacement cannot make a claim even if the original jobholder stays away for 11 weeks before confinement and the full 29 after (plus a possible extra four if unfit). It is still, however, important to make it clear to the replacement if they are being taken on in a temporary capacity, that such is the case.

There is no statutory right to paternity leave in the UK. However, paid paternity leave is being given by some employers, sometimes as the result of union pressure. The Equal Opportunities Commission is also encouraging its introduction.

Maternity pay A woman absent because of pregnancy or confinement will be entitled to receive maternity pay (which is taxable) and subject to national insurance contribution deductions for the first six weeks of her absence so long as she:

(a) has at least two years' service (or five years' if she works less than 16 but more than eight hours per week);

(b) continues to work up to 11 weeks before the beginning of the expected week of confinement; and

(c) informs her employer (in writing if he so requests) that she will be absent from work because of her pregnancy; this notice must be given at least 21 days before her absence begins (or as soon as reasonably practicable).

It would be wise for employers to bring this requirement to the attention of staff in the appropriate documentation.

Maternity pay is 90 per cent of a normal week's pay less the quite separate state maternity allowance (whether or not she is entitled to a full allowance). The employer can reclaim any maternity payments and his national insurance contributions paid on this from the Maternity Pay Fund, which is financed by the higher employers' social security contributions. Application forms for the refund are available from Department of Employment offices, and it is important that these forms *(Employee's Receipt for Maternity Pay)* are signed when the money is paid.

It should be noted that maternity pay is not dependent on returning to work following the birth of the child.

Dismissal A pregnant employee who has been working for her employer for 12 months (or five years if she works between 8 and 16 hours per week) may not be dismissed because of her pregnancy (or any reason connected with it) unless:

(a) her condition makes it impossible for her to do the job adequately;

(b) she cannot continue to work without contravening the law (eg because of exposure to X-rays).

Before a woman can be dismissed for one of these reasons the employer must see if there is a suitable alternative job to offer her. If she is dismissed because there is no alternative job she will retain the right to return to her job and to maternity pay. If she refuses an offer of suitable alternative work, she will be considered to have resigned, and lose her rights. Complaints about unfair dismissal, or failure to offer alternative employment, are heard by industrial tribunals.

10 Racial discrimination

P

The hotel and catering industry has for many years given employment to large numbers of staff with a wide variety of ethnic origins. Hoteliers and caterers in most parts of the UK also deal with a wide racial mix of customers. By and large, this has occurred without too many problems, though it should be noted that employers from the industry were amongst the first to be investigated by the Commission for Racial Equality (CRE) and served with non-discrimination notices. Considerable efforts continue to be made in this country to ensure that ethnic minority groups are not discriminated against, and that they have full opportunity to develop and use their talents and abilities for the benefit of us all.

The CRE has powers to conduct formal investigations and can assist an individual in taking a complaint to a court or an industrial tribunal. The CRE's *Code of Practice on Employment* advocates that employers adopt an equal opportunities policy to ensure that there is no unlawful discrimination and that equal opportunity is genuinely available; this should be clearly communicated to all staff.

Other recommendations (for full details see the code) are that employers should:

- allocate overall responsibility for the policy to a member of senior management
- discuss and where possible agree with trade union or employee representatives, the contents and implementation of the policy
- make sure that the policy is known to all employees and job applicants
- provide training for all supervisory staff and other relevant decision makers to ensure that they understand their responsibilities under the law and under company policy
- examine and regularly review existing procedures and criteria and, where they are found to be actually or potentially discriminatory, to change them
- make an initial analysis of the ethnic composition of the workforce to identify possible areas for action
- monitor the ethnic composition of the workforce and of job applicants on a regular basis in order to evaluate the progress of the policy.

†The Race
Relations Act
1976 applies
only to Great
Britain and not
Northern
Ireland.

The Race Relations Act 1976† permits employers in certain limited circumstances to take initiatives that will help to integrate members of racial minority groups into the workforce. For example, an employer with no, or disproportionately few, members of a racial minority group doing particular work may lawfully encourage members of that group to take advantage of opportunities for doing that work, and can run special training courses for existing employees of the racial groups in question.

Training has an important part to play in the maintenance of good race relations and training in the use of English can be particularly helpful to immigrant workers as well as to the employer. The HCITB has produced a guide to the analysis of communications training needs for ethnic minority groups, 'Qué?' This guide was produced with the co-operation of the Industrial Language Training Service. The ILTS provides in-company language training for racial minority group workers, and also provides communications and awareness training for managers, supervisors and trade union officials.

The keeping of ethnic staff records is also recommended by the CRE codes of practice, to enable more accurate monitoring of the situation.

11 Staff records

Staff are an important and expensive resource, the resource that brings all other investments – plant, equipment and premises – into profitable life. Staff records assist the effective use of staff by:

● cutting down the decisions that have to be made on the basis of guesswork

● enabling the detection and control of problems in recruitment, staff turnover, sickness, accidents, etc

● highlighting individual levels of performance that can be compared with the standards desired, which will assist in staff development.

Staff records also provide factual *written* information, for example of warnings, disciplinary matters, absence etc. If such information is kept 'in the head' of a manager, it is liable to be forgotten or muddled – worse, it is lost to the organisation if the manager leaves or is absent. Written records can also be vital in employment disputes (unfair dismissal cases etc) where they may form an important part of the evidence.

The type of records kept will depend on the size and nature of the business. Table 6 gives an example of the details most organisations will probably need to keep, and the free ACAS booklet *Personnel Records* (Advisory Booklet No 3) gives further advice and examples. The example of a labour analysis record sheet in Table 7 is reproduced from this booklet.

When designing a record system bear in mind the routine returns required by Government departments. Perhaps, for example, custom-built records can help save time in completing them, or one of the simple record systems available from a number of office equipment suppliers will be effective. Many of the computer systems now being installed can also be extended to cover personnel records, with restricted access to preserve confidentiality.

Finally, remember that whatever system is established, it needs to be not only accurate, up-to-date and reliable, but confidential and consistent.

Table 6
Staff records

For individual employees

1 Name.
2 Sex.
3 Next of kin.
4 Address.
5 Telephone number.
6 Date of birth.
7 Educational qualifications.
8 Whether registered disabled, and if so, disablement number.
9 Date of commencement.
10 Previous employment history.
11 Hours worked (especially if covered by a wages council).
12 Grade.
13 Wage rate, date of review and amount awarded.
14 Holidays (entitlement and days taken).
15 Sickness record (including details of sick pay).
16 Absence record.
17 Accident record.
18 Lateness record.
19 Disciplinary record (if applicable).
20 Training (eg courses attended).

For groups of employees

1 Staff turnover and stability analysed by department or job type (see Table 7).
2 Accident rate analysed by department.
3 Records of the racial/ethnic origin of employees, to enable a check to be made of how the organisation needs to act to ensure that all staff have equal opportunities.

Employee Relations

Table 7
Example of
labour analysis
record sheet

Department			Period		
Length of service	Sex	Left voluntarily	Dismissed	Redundant	Total
Less than 1 month	M				
	F				
1–3 months	M				
	F				
4–12 months	M				
	F				
1–5 years	M				
	F				
Total	M				
	F				

	M	F	Total
(a) Total employed at beginning of period			
(b) Total number of leavers during period			
(c) Total starters during period			
(d) Total employed at end of period			
(e) Average number employed during period, ie $\frac{(a) + (d)}{2}$			

Labour turnover (%)

$\dfrac{\text{Number of leavers during period} \times 100}{\text{Average employed during period}}$ ie $\dfrac{(b) \times 100}{(e)} =$

Labour Stability Index (%)

$\dfrac{\text{Number currently employed with 1 year's service or more} \times 100}{\text{Total number of employees 1 year ago}} =$

Acknowledgement: the above is taken from ACAS Advisory Booklet No 3

12 Developing your staff

One of the most important tasks a manager faces is that of getting the best out of his staff. This means helping them to carry out their present duties as effectively as possible and also working with them to enable them to take on other, perhaps more demanding duties, if this is possible.

The HCITB's companion book *Training Your Staff* considers in detail the advantages of training, how to improve training effectiveness and how to train the trainers. The latter subject is also catered for in the Board's series of *Trainer Skills* courses.

Staff appraisal

Undoubtedly most employers regularly appraise the performance of their staff, but it can often be an informal system, less likely to develop the best from their staff than a systematic approach.

It is not only important that the appraiser and appraisee understand the purpose of the process, but that they are trained in the techniques involved and that adequate time and attention is devoted to the process. It is also important that proper plans are made to ensure that action agreed at an appraisal interview does actually happen. Many otherwise excellent appraisal schemes have been discredited because of a lack of 'follow-up'.

The potential benefits of appraisal are varied but include:

- getting the best out of an individual in his present job
- helping to develop him for another job, if appropriate
- improving staff morale because the organisation is seen to care about staff progress
- forming the basis of a training plan and if appropriate a manpower development plan
- enabling realistic targets for achievement to be set (and previous targets to be regularly assessed)
- (for large organisations) a consistent approach to the development of staff across all divisions and units.

Although the basics of an appraisal system are simple, see Checklist 4, experience shows that there are common pitfalls when putting them into practice. These include:

- failure to demonstrate commitment to the scheme at senior level (junior staff take their cue from the boss)

59

- failure to train appraisees in what to expect (there are often very understandable worries about confidentiality of personal records and the use to which the scheme is put)
- an over reliance on paperwork (appraisal documents need to be acted on and regularly reviewed: not just filed)
- failure to persist with the introduction of the scheme, and see it through over a two or three year period (appraisal is no instant panacea, but a better, long term, way of working).

Checklist 4

Appraisal interview

Before the interview, has the appraiser:

1 Made himself familiar with any previous appraisal discussions?
2 Informed the appraisee of the forthcoming interview?
3 Briefed himself on the subject headings to be discussed?
4 Set aside time?
5 Arranged a quiet place and for there to be no interruptions?
6 Let the appraisee know the subject headings?
7 Geared his approach to appraisal so as to establish norms for action in the future rather than simply to review historical performance?

Before the interview, has the appraisee:

1 Been made familiar with the purpose of the meeting?
2 Been told the subject headings to be raised?
3 Had the opportunity to think about what he wants to discuss?

After the meeting have the appraiser and appraisee agreed:

1 A record of what has been discussed?
2 A programme to review and monitor plans and targets set?

13 Trade unions and the employer

Employees have the legal right to join a trade union and the Employment Protection (Consolidation) Act (Section 23) gives them protection against any discrimination or victimisation by their employer which is intended to prevent them from being, or seeking to become, a member of an independent trade union.

The EP(C)A also established new legal rights concerning disclosure of information, time off for union activity, and protection against dismissal because of union membership, but the provision concerning union recognition has now been repealed.

Recognising a trade union for collective bargaining

The process by which an employer agrees to deal with a trade union representing all or some of his staff, 'recognition', often starts with an agreement that the employer will deal with the union on disciplinary matters only. The scope of the agreement may then be gradually widened by mutual agreement to include such matters as:

- terms and conditions of employment, or the physical conditions in which any workers are required to work
- engagement or non-engagement, or termination or suspension of employment, or the duties of employment of one or more workers
- allocation of work or the duties of employment as between workers or groups of workers
- facilities for officials of trade unions
- machinery for negotiation or consultation, and other procedures relating to any of the foregoing matters, including the recognition by employers or employers' associations of the right of a trade union to represent workers in any such negotiation or consultation or in the carrying out of such procedures.

The decision whether or not to recognise a trade union is one that must not be taken lightly. An employer should be aware of the implications, and should find out the views of the staff involved.

The legal procedure whereby a union could request ACAS to investigate and, if appropriate, recommend that a union be recognised has now been repealed, though ACAS still have a duty to advise and conciliate in recognition cases, if invited to do so. Employers can also seek confidential advice from ACAS if they are faced with a request for union recognition or if they require assistance in drawing up a procedural agreement. It is thus left to employers and unions to arrive at a mutually acceptable arrangement as to when and if recognition is to be granted, and the range of matters to be covered by any such agreement.

If an employer decides to recognise a trade union for collective bargaining, it is not sensible to do so grudgingly. Far better to be positive and to work towards the development of an effective relationship, especially at a local level.

It is a good practice to make available appropriate facilities for the use of staff representatives. This might take the form of access to administrative facilities, notification of engagement of new employees, access to a telephone etc, in order to help the representatives to be more effective, both to the staff they represent, and, thus also, to their employer. ACAS code of practice No 3 *Time Off for Trade Union Duties and Activities* gives further information.

Trade union immunities

When employees go on strike or take other forms of industrial action, they will usually, by doing so, be in breach of their contracts of employment. This means that when trade unions or trade union officials call for industrial action they are in practice calling on the employees concerned to break their contracts. The same is true of an individual picket who tries to persuade others not to go into work or not to deliver or collect goods. Both organisers and individual pickets may also be interfering with the ability of the employer of the employees and of other employers to fulfil their commercial contracts.

†The common law underlies much of the law of this country. It is basically case-law (developed by the courts) as opposed to statute law passed by Parliament.

Under the common law† it is unlawful to induce people to break their contracts or to interfere with the performance of a contract or to threaten to do either of these things. This means that without some special protection, trade unions or trade union officials might face the possibility of legal action for inducing breaches of contract every time they called a strike.

Trade union immunities were introduced into legislation to stop this happening. They provide, in effect, that trade unions and individuals cannot, in certain circumstances, be sued for inducing breaches of contract. In other words they can call industrial action without fear of being sued in the courts.

The circumstances covered by the immunities have been much widened over the years. By the late 1970s most calls for industrial action were protected, even though such industrial action might inflict a great deal of damage on industry and the community. The Employment Acts 1980 and 1982 have sought to reverse this process. They have withdrawn immunities from the organisation of certain types of industrial action so that in some cases trade unions and their officials may once again face legal proceedings for inducing breaches of contract.

The details are described below.

Two further points are important to an understanding of the law governing strikes and other industrial action:

(a) Trade union immunities protect those who persuade others to break their contracts: they do *not* protect those who by going on strike break their own contracts. This means that even where the organisers of strikes can claim legal immunity, the individual striker may face disciplinary action for breaking his contract. An employee may even be taken to court by his employer and sued for breach of contract—although this rarely happens;

†Except in the case of the police, the armed forces and merchant seamen when they are at sea.

(b) Trade union immunities are primarily concerned with the *civil* not the *criminal* law. It is not a criminal offence to strike†. But if in the course of a strike someone commits a criminal offence (for example, by assaulting another person or damaging someone's property), he has no special protection and is just as liable to be prosecuted by the police as any other member of the public.

No special immunity for trade unions

In the past, trade unions have had a much wider immunity from legal actions than trade union officials or other individuals. This not only protected them from legal proceedings if they organised unlawful industrial action. It also prevented them from being sued in certain circumstances if they committed other unlawful acts like negligence, nuisance, breach of duty and defamation.

This special immunity for trade unions (which was contained in Section 14 of the Trade Union and Labour Relations Act 1974) has been abolished by the Employment Act 1982. This means that the immunity for trade unions and individuals is exactly the same. Or to put it another way it is now possible to seek injunctions against, and sue for damages, trade unions, as well as individuals, if they commit the unlawful acts (for example, negligence, nuisance) described above, or if they organise unlawful industrial action.

The law does not protect those organising industrial action and those taking part in picketing from being sued for inducing breaches of contract if:

- the action is not in contemplation or furtherance of a trade dispute
- the action is unlawful secondary action
- the action constitutes secondary picketing
- the action is being taken against persons because they employ non-union (or union) labour or because they do not recognise a union
- those concerned commit unlawful acts other than inducing breaches of contract.

Trade disputes

There is a detailed legal definition of what constitutes a trade dispute in Section 29 of the Trade Union and Labour Relations Act 1974. Basically, however, there are two main conditions which must be satisfied:

(a) there must be a dispute between workers and their own employer†; *and*

(b) the dispute must be wholly or mainly about such matters as their pay and conditions, jobs, allocation of work, discipline, negotiating machinery and trade union membership (the full list is contained in Section 29(1) of the TULRA.

Several types of dispute, which were previously lawful, are now, as a result of the EA82, *excluded* from the definition of a lawful trade dispute. These include:

● disputes between groups of workers or between trade unions, where no employer is involved in the dispute

● disputes between workers and employers other than their own

● disputes between a trade union and an employer, where none of that employer's workforce are in dispute with him

● disputes which have only *a connection* with matters like pay and conditions and are not *wholly or mainly* about such matters

● disputes which relate to matters occurring overseas (except where workers taking action in this country in support of the dispute are likely to be affected by its outcome).

Secondary industrial action

'Secondary action' is defined in Section 17 of the Employment Act 1980 as being the organisation of industrial action taken by workers (in breach of their contracts of employment) whose employer is not a party to the trade dispute. For example, if there is a dispute between an employer and his workforce at an establishment, action by workers of *another* employer to support the workers in dispute will usually constitute secondary action.

Where such action interferes with the performance of *commercial* contracts, or threatens to do so, its organisers have no protection from legal proceedings unless all four of the conditions below are satisfied:

(a) the workers involved in the secondary action work for a customer or supplier of the employer in dispute;

(b) that supplier or customer has a current commercial contract with the employer in dispute;

(c) the principal purpose of the secondary action is directly to prevent or disrupt supplies to or from the employer in dispute during the dispute;

(d) the secondary action is likely to achieve that purpose.

Broadly, this means that secondary action is only lawful where it is taken by those who work for a supplier or a customer of the employer in dispute and the action is directed at the business being conducted between the supplier or customer and the employer in dispute. If the secondary action is indiscriminate in its effects—for example, if its principal effect is to disrupt the business of other employers, not involved in the dispute—then its organisers have no immunity and may be liable to legal proceedings brought by those damaged.

Associated employers

There are special provisions to cover the situation where because of a dispute the employer in dispute transfers work normally done by his or her own employees to an associated employer, such as a subsidiary company. In such circumstances the organisation of industrial action by workers at the associated company, or at their customers or their suppliers will be lawful only if both the conditions below are satisfied:

(a) the principal purpose of the action is to prevent or disrupt the supply of goods or services which but for the dispute would have been supplied by or to the employer in dispute;

(b) the action is likely to achieve that purpose.

Secondary picketing

There is also no legal protection for those who organise or take part in secondary picketing—that is, picketing at a place other than the picket's own place of work. This is so whether or not the picketing is in contemplation or furtherance of a trade dispute.

What constitutes lawful picketing is defined in Section 15 of the TULRA as amended by Section 16 of the Employment Act 1980. This provides that picketing is now lawful only if:

● the person is picketing at or near his own place of work

● the purpose of the picketing is peacefully to obtain or communicate information, or peacefully to persuade a person to work or not to work.

There are three exceptions to the requirement that a person may picket lawfully only at or near his own place of work. These are as follow:

(a) a trade union official may accompany a member of his union whom he represents so long as the member is picketing at his own place of work;

(b) a person, (for example, a mobile worker) who does not normally work at one particular place, or for whom it is impracticable to picket at his actual place of work, may picket at the premises of the employer from which he works or from which the work is administered;

(c) a person who is not in employment may picket at his former place of work in contemplation or furtherance of a trade dispute, but only if the termination of his employment with the employer gave rise to or is connected with the dispute in support of which he is picketing.

Where picketing does not satisfy the conditions set out above it has no legal immunity and the pickets or their organisers may be taken to court by those who are damaged by the picketing. Picketing which is not peaceful—for example, if it involves violent or abusive behaviour or involves obstruction of the highway—may also be a criminal offence; and in such circumstances those responsible may be arrested and prosecuted by the police.

More detailed information about the law on picketing is contained in the code of practice: *Picketing* issued under the powers given to the Secretary of State for Employment in Section 3 of the Employment Act 1980. This outlines the law on picketing and gives practical guidance on its conduct. Copies are available free of charge from Jobcentres, employment offices and unemployment benefit offices.

Industrial action against non-union firms

Another type of industrial action for which there is no protection—regardless of the existence of a trade dispute—is that taken against employers simply because they are employing non-union (or union) labour or because they do not recognise a trade union. These provisions are part of wider measures to protect non-union firms.

Other unlawful acts

Where there is legal immunity for those who organise industrial action or take part in picketing, that immunity only protects them from legal action for inducing breaches of contract or threatening to do so. This means that there is no immunity for strikers or pickets or their organisers who commit other civil wrongs or criminal offences, and if such wrongs or offences are committed at the same time as inducement to breach a contract, then even the immunity for that inducement may be lost.

So if, for example, strikers or pickets commit an unlawful trespass, they are just as liable to be sued for that and any other unlawful acts involved (including inducing breaches of contract) as any other members of the public who occupy premises unlawfully. This point was underlined by the repeal in EA82 of Section 13(2) of the TULRA, which it had recently been suggested might in certain circumstances have given protection to those involved in sit-ins.

Remedies

There are basically two remedies available to those who go to court about unlawful industrial action.

First, those damaged can seek a court order to prevent the action or have it stopped. If the case is urgent, courts may grant such an order on an interim basis without waiting for a full hearing of the case. However, the unions or individuals against whom the order is sought have the legal right to be

66

given a chance to put their case. If an order is made but disobeyed, those who sought it can go back to court and seek to have those concerned declared in 'contempt of court'. Anyone found to be in contempt of court may face fines or even imprisonment.

Second, it is possible to claim damages from those responsible for unlawful acts. Such cases must go to a full hearing of the case which will usually be at a later date. An action for damages may be preceded by an application for an order. But there is no requirement that it should do so.

Trade union membership rights

Since 1971 the law has protected the rights of individuals to join trade unions and to take part in their activities. However, before the 1980 and 1982 Employment Acts the legal protection for people who did *not* want to belong to trade unions was very limited and there was virtually no protection at all for the non-union employee in a closed shop. As a result of these Acts, the protection for those who do not want to belong to a trade union has been greatly increased.

Rights of trade union members

†An appropriate time means, broadly, a time when the employee has the employer's permission to take part in these activities or any time when the employee is not required to be at work, such as lunch-times.

As the law now stands employees are entitled to a remedy from an industrial tribunal if:
- they are dismissed or are selected for redundancy because they belong, or propose to belong, to a trade union or because they have been taking part in trade union activities at an appropriate time,† *or*
- they have some other action taken against them, as individuals, to prevent or deter them from belonging to a trade union or from taking part in union activities at an appropriate time—or as a penalty for so doing.

Rights of non-union members in a closed shop

A closed shop is an agreement between an employer and one or more trade unions which requires certain employees to be members of a trade union. Such agreements may not be written down: they are often a matter of custom and practice.

The Employment Acts 1980 and 1982 have not made closed shops unlawful but they have greatly extended the protection for non-union employees covered by such agreements. The most important change is that from November 1, 1984, every closed shop will be subject to the test of a secret ballot. After that date anyone who is dismissed because he is not a union member in a closed shop which has not been approved in a secret ballot will be entitled to a remedy from a tribunal.

Other closed shop protection

The Employment Acts 1980 and 1982 provide protection for non-union employees in a wide range of specific cases. These forms of protection apply and will continue to apply after November 1, 1984, even if a closed shop has been approved in a secret ballot. They cover:

(a) employees who genuinely object on grounds of conscience or other deeply held personal conviction to being a member of any trade union whatsoever or of a particular union;

(b) employees who were already employed before the closed shop agreement covering their jobs took effect and who have at no time subsequently been members of a trade union in accordance with the agreement;

(c) employees who work under a closed shop agreement which took effect after August 14, 1980, who were entitled to vote in the first ballot under which the closed shop agreement was approved, and who have not since then been members of a trade union in accordance with the agreement;

(d) employees who at the time of dismissal *either* had been found by an industrial tribunal to have been unreasonably excluded or expelled from the trade union which they were required to join under the closed shop agreement (see opposite) *or* who had a complaint of unreasonable exclusion or expulsion by that union pending before a tribunal (this does not apply, however, if by the time of dismissal: the industrial tribunal's decision has been overturned on appeal; *or* the employee has become a member of the union concerned at some point after making his complaint to the tribunal; *or* the employee has turned down a chance of rejoining the union since making his complaint); *and*

(e) employees who have qualifications relating to their jobs which make them subject to a written code of conduct and who *either* have been expelled from their trade union because they refused to strike or take other industrial action on the grounds that this would have breached their code of conduct; *or* who have refused to belong to the union concerned on the grounds that membership would have required them to take industrial action in breach of the code.

Other rights for non-union members

Whether they work in a closed shop or not, all employees are entitled to a remedy from a tribunal if they are selected for redundancy because they do not belong to a trade union. And where there is no closed shop all employees are similarly entitled to a remedy if they are dismissed because they do not belong to a trade union or if they have some other action taken against them to compel them to join a union.

Remedies

The remedy which a tribunal will provide in all these cases involving membership or non-membership of a union depends on the employer's action. If the employer has dismissed the employee concerned he will either be ordered to take the employee back or to pay compensation. In the latter case, as a result of EA82, compensation will normally be much higher than in other unfair dismissal cases. In addition, where dismissal (other than because of redundancy) has occurred a tribunal can be asked for an order of interim relief pending a full hearing. This is an order requiring the employee's contract to be continued until then. Applications for interim relief must be made within seven days of dismissal.

If the employee has not been dismissed but has suffered some other action by the employer the tribunal will make a declaration to this effect and may also award compensation. Applications to a tribunal in any of these cases must normally be made within three months of the dismissal or other action concerned.

Trade union liability over union membership issues

Under the common law it has always been possible for union members to take their union to court if they think that the union has broken its own rules in some way. One example might be where a union disciplines a member for doing something which the rule book says he is allowed to do. However, this safeguard provides no protection against unions which treat their members unreasonably but do so within their rules. The Employment Acts 1980 and 1982 have therefore provided remedies against unions which act unreasonably either in expelling or refusing to admit a member or in putting pressure on an employer to dismiss or take other action against non-union employees.

Unreasonable exclusion or expulsion from a union

Under rights given by EA82, employees who work in a closed shop or who are seeking work in one are entitled to a remedy from a tribunal if they are unreasonably expelled or excluded from the union which the closed shop requires them to join. In deciding whether someone is entitled to this remedy a tribunal will consider not just whether the union has acted in accordance with its own rules but also all the other circumstances surrounding the union's action, including its fairness. The tribunal will also consider guidance in the code of practice: *Closed Shop Agreements and Arrangements* (issued under EA82) if it thinks this relevant. This guidance covers such issues as when a union ought not to discipline members who refuse to strike. If a tribunal decides that a person has been unreasonably expelled or excluded from a union it will declare that this has happened—a clear indication to the union that it must now admit or re-admit the person concerned—and may later award compensation. A complaint to a tribunal of unreasonable exclusion or expulsion must normally be made within six months of the action concerned.

Union pressure on employers to dismiss non-members

An employer who takes action (whether dismissal or action short of dismissal) against a non-union employee may do so because of pressure, in the form of actual or threatened industrial action, exerted by a trade union because the employee was not a member of a trade union. In such a case the employer or the employee concerned can require the union involved to be 'joined' (that is, brought in as a party) to any tribunal proceedings. If the tribunal decides to award the employee compensation and finds that the union did, indeed, put such pressure on the employer it may order the union to pay some or all of its award of compensation to the person concerned.

Union labour only and union recognition requirements

The Employment Act 1982 has prohibited companies, local authorities and others from imposing on contractors what have become known as *union labour only requirements* and *recognition requirements*. These are requirements which make it a condition of getting onto a tender list or of obtaining a contract that the contractor employs only trade union members or recognises, negotiates or consults with trade unions. The effect of such requirements is to exclude non-union businesses—particularly small firms and self-employed people—from obtaining contracts. The Act:

(a) declared void union labour only and recognition requirements in contracts;

(b) made it a breach of statutory duty to impose such requirements in the drawing up of tender lists and the awarding of contracts;

(c) removed the legal immunities from trade union pressure to impose and enforce such requirements;

(d) removed the legal immunities from the organisation of other industrial action which interferes with goods and services from non-union sources.

Industrial action against non-union businesses

The Employment Act 1982 also deals more generally with trade union action against businesses which do or do not employ union labour or which do not recognise, negotiate or consult with trade unions or trade union officials.

As a result of the Act, a trade union or individual who organises or threatens industrial action (in breach of contracts of employment) will have no legal immunity and may face legal proceedings if the industrial action interferes with the supply (whether or not under a contract) of goods or services or can reasonably be expected to have that effect; *and* the reason or one of the reasons for that action is *either*:

● that work done or to be done in connection with the supply of the goods or services has been, or is likely to be, done by persons employed by another employer who are or are not union members; *or*

● the supplier of the goods or services (that is, in practice, the contractor) does not recognise, negotiate, or consult with trade unions or trade union officials.

Some examples of the type of industrial action which may be affected by this provision are:

(a) the refusal of employees to handle goods from another firm because the goods were produced by non-union employees;

(b) trade union blacking of the goods and services of a firm and its customers because the firm does not recognise a trade union for collective bargaining;

(c) the refusal of workers to work with another employer's workers or to allow them to enter a place of work because they do not have the requisite union card.

The effect of removing the legal immunities, in these cases, is to give to those who are or may be damaged by the unlawful industrial action the right to seek an order against the trade union or individual who is organising it to restrain their unlawful acts, and to sue them for damages.

Trade union secret ballots

The Employment Act 1980 contains two provisions to encourage trade unions to make greater use of secret ballots.

Firstly it enables payments to be made out of public funds towards the costs which an independent trade union incurs in holding postal ballots for certain purposes. These purposes are:

● calling or ending a strike or other industrial action

● accepting or rejecting a proposal by an employer on pay and certain other related matters

● electing trade union officials in accordance with the union's rules

● amending the union's rules

● ballots under the Trade Union (Amalgamations etc) Act 1964.

The Certification Officer for Trade Unions and Employers' Associations is responsible for the administration of the public funds.

Secondly, an employer with more than 20 workers can be requested by an independent trade union which he recognises for collective bargaining purposes to provide a place on his premises where the members may vote in a secret ballot. If the employer refuses then the union can complain to an industrial tribunal and may be awarded compensation.

A substantial section of Chapter 13 has been reproduced from the Department of Employment booklet *Employment Acts 1980 and 1982, an Outline.* The HCITB would like to acknowledge the Department's assistance in allowing its material to be used in this way.

14 Communication and consultation with employees

Any discussion about the improvement of employee relations is likely to include reference to the importance of effective communication between staff and management, and between different departments in an organisation.

In recent years, the adoption of regular and systematic forms of staff consultation has also been advocated, and there has been much discussion about the potential benefits of a greater participation by staff in the running 'or joint regulation' of the enterprise.

It is not possible here to explore fully the merits of different systems or approaches to communication, consultation, or participation. A careful assessment should be carried out, embracing the whole circumstances of an organisation and the expectations of its staff, taking into account:

- the history of employee relations in the organisation
- the requirements of employment law
- expectations and attitudes of staff and management.

The following notes are therefore intended to give an introduction to the approaches taken by some organisations.

Joint consultation

This is the process by which employers and employees discuss, before decisions are taken, matters affecting the efficiency of the enterprise and the interests of the employees to which representatives can contribute. It is generally carried out by committees, incorporating trade union representatives if applicable, with an agreed constitution.

In an industry as personalised as the hotel and catering industry, management and staff meet frequently during the working day with the opportunity to exchange views and ideas. The process of joint consultation is a way of *systematising* this process, allowing the exploration of views and ideas *before* managers take decisions.

Consultation is *not* the same as negotiation – it does not involve any attempt to strike bargains where matters are in dispute. Whereas negotiation involves a process of give and take so as to reach a mutually acceptable solution or decision, consultation is, rather, a free exchange of views on matters which affect staff, as a result of which management will be able to make better informed decisions.

The three main achievements of joint consultation are usually held to be that:

(a) there is an improvement in the quality of management decisions and of the working life of staff because the views, experience and ideas of staff are taken into account before decisions are made;

(b) when staff have been given the opportunity to contribute at the formative stage of management decisions (especially where changes are involved), they are more likely to co-operate whole-heartedly with any action resulting from decisions subsequently taken by management;

(d) much misunderstanding and mistrust is avoided by providing informal discussions to clarify issues before decisions are reached.

Experience shows that while it is known that considerable training is generally required when a consultative committee is set up, both for management (in the effective conduct of joint consultation meetings), and for staff (in the use of the system), in reality inadequate attention is given to it. Patience is also needed; there will always be teething troubles. Further details can be obtained from the Industrial Society, or from HCITB regional offices.

Communication   It is a truism to say that 'communications in most organisations are vital to good performance'. Everyone agrees that this is so, yet imperfect communications continue to cause disputes and other problems.

One technique which has been adopted successfully to pass information swiftly through an organisation is that of 'briefing groups' or 'team briefing'. The use of these groups is said to:
- increase commitment of staff to their jobs
- clearly identify and support the team leader
- reduce the number of misunderstandings that take place
- increase the ability to achieve co-operation when introducing a change
- lessen the damaging effect of rumour (the grapevine always denigrates management – usually without foundation).

A written brief is prepared detailing the information that needs to be passed on. This brief incorporates the essential items of information, and suggested answers to questions that may arise. The first group to meet (usually at a senior level) is given the brief and each member of this group then becomes the leader of a group at the next lower level. The process is repeated as often as is necessary, keeping the number of levels as few as possible.

For effective briefing it is important that:
- the manager or supervisor briefs the group face to face
- the group is kept to a manageable size
- briefings are regular and relevant
- understanding is monitored

- close attention is paid to the 'starting up' problems of briefing groups
- the system is monitored to ensure that briefings are being held as planned.

The process enables speedy, accurate transmission of information and involves all levels, including supervisors, who otherwise often tend to be left out. It does not replace consultation or negotiation, but enables management to tell employees of developments as necessary. It also provides some degree of feedback to management, via the questions raised by staff.

There are many other means of communicating with staff – notice boards, company newsletters, audio visual presentations, and attitude surveys, to name a few. For guidance, contact your local ACAS or HCITB office.

Employee participation and involvement

In 1972 the EEC introduced a draft Fifth Directive on the harmonisation of company law. In addition to a number of company law provisions, it proposed that employees be represented on the supervisory board of a two-tier board system in public limited companies with over 500 employees. Following consideration of these original proposals, a revised text was produced in July 1983. This would apply to public limited companies with more than 1,000 employees (counting also the employees of subsidiaries) and would offer a wider choice of structures for employee participation.

In 1980, the EEC also introduced a draft directive on procedures for informing and consulting employees (known as the *Vredeling Directive*). A revised text was issued in July 1983 which, like the first, would, if implemented, require head offices of organisations employing 1,000 or more workers within the EEC (including multinationals) to inform and consult employees in subsidiaries or separate establishments through local management.

Both draft directives have now been referred to working groups of officials from capitals for detailed examination and consideration, and it is expected to be a number of years before final decisions from member states are needed.

In Britain, both the Government and the CBI have urged companies to voluntarily develop schemes for worker participation and consultation, believing that successful employee involvement depends as much on a spirit of co-operation as on the existence of formal machinery. The TUC has also played an active role, through the European Trade Union Confederation, in seeking the adoption of an instrument such as the Fifth Directive, and has welcomed the proposal, by the EEC, for information and consultation rights in complex and international corporations.

In addition, the Employment Act 1982 requires, for companies employing 250 or more staff, that the directors' annual report – under Section 16 of the Companies Act 1967 – must contain a statement of the steps taken to introduce, maintain, or develop arrangements concerned with employee involvement in the running of the company, describing the action taken in the previous year.

15 Disciplinary rules, procedures and grievances

The Employment Protection (Consolidation) Act (Sections 1–5) requires that the written particulars of employment, to be given to each employee, must specify:

(a) disciplinary rules applicable to the employee;

(b) a person to whom the employee can apply if he is dissatisfied with any disciplinary decision referring to him, or if he seeks redress of any grievance relating to his employment;

(c) how such an application should be made;

(d) any steps following from such an application.

If an employer fails to provide the information required, he can face a complaint before an industrial tribunal. However, if a problem reaches a tribunal on another matter, for example unfair dismissal, the failure to have an adequate grievance/disciplinary procedure will be a serious disadvantage to the employer when the case is considered.

Some rules and procedures are necessary for the effective operation of any organisation. Without them, inconsistency and unfairness are likely to occur. Thus it is sensible to anticipate and prevent the occurrence of problems and misunderstandings by drawing up and implementing a comprehensive set of rules and procedures for the organisation.

Drawing up a disciplinary procedure

The ACAS *Code of Practice on Disciplinary Practice and Procedures in Employment,* which is reproduced in Appendix V, gives general guidance on the approach to be adopted. Note particularly:

(a) The small firm is required to adopt the same general approach as the larger employer, though 'it may not be practicable to adopt all the detailed provisions'. Tribunals are now required to take account of the size, and administrative resources, of an employer, when assessing the fairness of a decision to dismiss.

(b) Rules 'should not be so general as to be meaningless'.

(c) Penalties attached to breach of the rules should be made clear and, in particular, employees should be given 'a clear indication of the type of conduct which may warrant summary dismissal' (ie dismissal without notice).

(d) Management has the duty of ensuring that employees *understand* the rules, for example, by explaining rules to staff, especially at induction.

(e) The comments on suspension, see paragraph 12(c) of the Code.

(f) If the employer intends to change an existing system, or to introduce a new one, he should discuss and agree the proposals with employees or their representatives beforehand.

(g) Investigations should always be carried out before taking any disciplinary action, even summary dismissal, and 'before a decision is made or penalty imposed the individual should be interviewed and given the opportunity to state his or her case'. The way in which a disciplinary interview is carried out is important and may usefully form the basis for training to develop the necessary level of skill. Table 8 overleaf suggests an approach.

Grievances

Individual grievances are usually dealt with by a procedure separate from the disciplinary appeals procedure (see paragraph 16 of the *Code of Practice*). It is, in any event necessary to have a clearly defined process for dealing with grievances.

Make sure that grievance/disciplinary procedures are known, understood and followed, both by those operating them and those to whom they apply, and that penalties for breach of procedures are clearly defined. Hasty ill-considered decisions are dangerous.

Employee Relations

Table 8
Disciplinary
interview

Before the interview

1 Suspend the employee, if desirable and legally possible.
2 Establish the facts; do not accept hearsay evidence.
3 Establish the name and background of the offender, date and time of offence.
4 Obtain the relevant records of employment.
5 Don't delay unnecessarily.
6 Get statements/witnesses if appropriate, but without delay.
7 Find out about precedent/other similar cases.
8 Tell employee the purpose of the interview and allow him to bring a representative, if he wishes.
9 Arrange for the interview to be held at a time and place that suits both parties best and see to it that it is not interrupted.

During the interview

1 Start the interview by letting the employee know the general charge and specific details of the offence.
2 Avoid giving the impression that the employer has already 'made up his mind'.
3 Stick completely to work behaviour and avoid all reference to personalities. Conduct the interview in a factual fashion without emotion or anger.
4 Give the employee the opportunity to state his case.
5 Listen and note.
6 Keep control of the interview. Stick to the points at issue.
7 Throughout the interview provide opportunities for the offender to admit his shortcomings.
8 Decide action.
9 Give a decision or say when it will be given.

After the interview

1 Confirm in writing, and to representative if appropriate, the decision taken.
2 Keep a record.
3 Do not harbour a grudge against the person disciplined. The person required discipline and he received it. Give him the benefit of real hope that it has achieved its true purpose and by both word and action let him know that you consider it a thing of the past.

16 Dismissal

Dismissing a member of staff deprives him of his livelihood and is costly to the employer (who has to get a replacement, with all the disruption and effort that this entails). In addition, legal protection given to individual employees means that if the dismissal is shown to be 'unfair', the employer can lose a considerable amount of money in compensation, and can be required to re-employ or reinstate him (see Chapter 2).

Dismissal is no longer an easy way out of an employment difficulty. It is a final and expensive last resort to be used only when the situation really demands it and when the discipline/grievance procedures have been exhausted.

Unfair dismissal

Every member of staff has a right 'not to be unfairly dismissed by his employer' and 'a complaint may be presented to an industrial tribunal by any person, that he was unfairly dismissed by the employer', EP(C)A. When such a claim is made, the ex-employee has to show that he has been dismissed, and that he qualifies to make a claim for unfair dismissal. For his part, the employer has to show that he has a valid reason for the dismissal. The tribunal has to decide whether 'the employer acted reasonably or unreasonably in treating it as a sufficient reason for dismissing the employee; and that question shall be determined in accordance with equity and the substantial merits of the case' and is required to take account of 'the size and administrative resources of the employer's undertaking' in coming to a decision.

Section 57 of the Employment Protection (Consolidation) Act lists the reasons acceptable as 'potentially valid':

(a) capability: the inability to carry out the work he was engaged to do, for example because of sickness, lack of skill, technical, or academic qualifications;

(b) conduct;

(c) illegality (eg employing a driver without a licence, or a foreign worker without a work permit);

(d) true redundancy (see Chapter 17);

(e) other substantial reason.

The Act also lists reasons that will definitely be classed as 'unfair', including dismissal caused by:

(a) being a member of an independent trade union, or proposing to join one;

79

(b) taking part, or proposing to take part, in independent trade union activities at an appropriate time (outside work hours or during time agreed by the employer for union activity);

(c) refusing to join or remain in a non-independent trade union (see definition in Appendix I).

The introduction of the concept of unfair dismissal has been interpreted by many as meaning that it is now virtually impossible to dismiss an employee. This is emphatically untrue. If there is a *valid* reason for dismissal, an employee can be fairly dismissed at any time. Good disciplinary procedures, clear rules, accurate records all play a part in the process.

Claiming unfair dismissal

Any employee can claim he has been unfairly dismissed provided that:

(a) He works 16 hours per week or more (eight hours per week if the employee has five years' or more service).

(b) He is not over the normal retirement age for that organisation. The generally accepted retirement ages are at present 65 (men) and 60 (women). Where an organisation has different retirement arrangements these should be clearly stated, to avoid confusion.

(c) He has completed one year's service or would have completed this service at the expiry of his notice. This period is extended to two years for staff in small firms provided that at no time during that period did the number of employees employed by the employer, added to the number employed by any associated employer, exceed 20. In this, as in most employment matters, the period of employment must be continuous, ie unbroken. In general, an employee's service is presumed to have been continuous unless there is proof to the contrary. See Department of Employment booklet *Continuous Employment and a Week's Pay* for details.

Note that:

(a) claims for unfair dismissal on grounds of sex or race discrimination, or trade union activity, or in connection with a union membership agreement can be brought immediately without the one/two years qualification period;

(b) claims for dismissal because of a reason such as trade union membership or activity can be brought after retirement age.

Constructive dismissal

An employee can be regarded as having been dismissed if he terminates his own contract because his employer's behaviour is such that the employee feels that the employment contract has been breached or repudiated. For example, if the work an employee is required to do is drastically changed without his prior agreement, or if his terms of employment are changed, for example by the withdrawal of some allowances and privileges an employee *may* be entitled to resign and claim that he has been 'constructively' dismissed.

Case law has now given clear guidance on this matter: Lord Denning, when Master of the Rolls, said 'an employee is entitled to treat himself as constructively dismissed if the employer is guilty of conduct which is a significant breach going to the root of the contract of employment . . . the employee in those circumstances is entitled to leave without notice or to give notice . . . if he continues for any length of time without leaving, he will be regarded as having elected to affirm the contract and will lose his right to treat himself as discharged'.

It is sensible to protect organisations by making managers and supervisors aware of the nature of constructive dismissal, and by ensuring that employees who leave are interviewed to establish the reason for their departure.

If it is necessary to change any of the terms or conditions of employment of your staff, it is in any case good practice to consult and agree this with staff rather than attempt to impose the change unilaterally.

Wrongful dismissal

An employee is wrongfully dismissed if not given the proper period of notice (or wages in lieu) or if he has not received holiday pay, sick pay, or other benefits to which he is entitled under his contract of employment (see Chapter 7) unless he has so seriously misconducted himself as to 'repudiate his contract' (that is, indicated an intention not to be bound by his contractual duties) in which case he can be summarily dismissed. Stealing from a customer, or a flagrant breach of hygiene rules, might constitute grounds for summary dismissal, without notice or pay in lieu of notice. Even where summary dismissal is warranted the case must be properly investigated, and the employee given a chance to put his side of the story, before a decision is taken. The burden of showing that the employee has 'repudiated' his contract lies with the employer and such wrongful dismissal cases are dealt with by civil courts (County or High Court). Even if successful in dealing with a wrongful dismissal, an employer can still face a claim for compensation for unfair dismissal brought through an industrial tribunal.

If an employer summarily dismisses an employee, but to avoid ill-will decides to make some payment to him, short of paying his notice pay, it is sensible to ensure that the organisation's position is protected against a possible 'unfair dismissal' claim by sending a note with the payment saying that it is made 'without prejudice' to the company's right to dismiss summarily.

Avoiding problems

There are a number of steps managers and supervisors can take to protect the organisation from problems and perhaps unfair dismissal cases that reach an industrial tribunal. The conduct of disciplinary interviews is important (see Table 8). Other good personnel practices include:

(a) Never dismiss in anger.

(b) Get a second opinion before dismissing any employee who is eligible to claim unfair dismissal.

(c) If necessary, suspend the employee on full pay whilst investigating the circumstances, before making a decision.

(d) If possible, do not dismiss without the presence of a witness.

(e) Follow an agreed discipline/dismissal procedure, which should contain provision for at least one written warning before dismissal (see Appendix V).

(f) Keep a record of all warnings, even verbal ones. The time limit for making a complaint is three months from the date of termination but tribunals have discretion to hear complaints out of time where it was not reasonably practicable for the complaint to be made earlier.

(g) Make sure you understand the regulations on maternity leave, etc (see Chapter 9).

An employee not performing to the required standard should be dealt with according to whatever company procedure has been established. The points covered might include:

(a) Make sure that the required level of performance has been agreed with him.

(b) Bring specific instances of poor performance to the employee's notice.

(c) Give him the opportunity to improve, and assistance in doing so within a stated period.

(d) If, despite these efforts, no improvement occurs, dismiss the employee, using the disciplinary procedure as appropriate.

Dismissing

If it is necessary to dismiss an employee, the Employment Protection (Consolidation) Act (Section 53) requires an employer to give a dismissed employee, on request, a statement of the reasons for dismissal. The employee must have been employed for six months and the statement must be provided within 14 days of the request, which need not be made in writing. (Make sure that there is no chance of a verbal request being overlooked.)

The statement should be worded carefully, referring if possible to written warnings already given: it is admissible as evidence in any proceedings, including unfair dismissal cases. For example:

I refer you to memos dated.............................. and..............................
(copies of which you received) in which I warned you that if the conduct complained of continued I would have no alternative other than to dismiss you. (The conduct in

question was *[describe it]*). The reason for your dismissal was the continuation of that conduct in spite of warnings.

If an employer refuses to provide a statement a complaint may be made to an industrial tribunal, which if it upholds the complaint:

- may make a declaration as to what it finds were the reasons for dismissal
- shall make an award for the employers to pay a sum equal to two weeks' pay to the ex-employee.

If asked to give a reference on someone who has been dismissed, it is in an employer's own interests to make sure that the reference does not conflict with the dismissal. An interesting tribunal decision indicated that employers 'cannot have it both ways', that is giving a good reference, even if it is intended to help the ex-employee, whilst having sacked him for some serious offence. This should help employers to believe in the references they receive, too!

Employers are not legally obligated to provide a reference, though it is normal practice to do so on request. But as indicated above, if given, it should be accurate.

Taking a dismissal case to a tribunal

Tribunal cases are usually initiated by an employee (or ex-employee) who feels that he has been wrongly dealt with and applies to the tribunal for a decision, see Table 9. The employee completes an *Originating Application to an Industrial Tribunal* (Form IT1) which is sent to the Central Office of Industrial Tribunals, who send photocopies to the employer named and to ACAS, together with explanatory notes and a form for reply. It is important to ensure that the person receiving such correspondence in an organisation knows how to deal with it and that a reply is sent within the 14 day time limit. If this is not done the organisation may lose the right to have its side of the case heard.

When the employer's reply has been received (or even before this, if appropriate) the Conciliation Officer appointed by ACAS may contact the parties involved, or may be called in by them, to attempt to reach an agreed settlement. Information given to a Conciliation Officer by either of the parties involved is treated in confidence, and is not admissible as evidence in a tribunal case except with the consent of the person giving the information. Conciliation is a very useful process that greatly reduces the number of cases actually reaching an industrial tribunal. In 1982 some 33,109 applications were disposed of by tribunals but 65 per cent did not in fact reach a hearing having been conciliated, voluntarily settled or otherwise withdrawn.

Conciliation should therefore be seriously considered as an alternative to allowing the case to proceed. This decision should be based on a mature consideration of the strengths and weaknesses of the case. Whilst it may be tempting to proceed if

Employee Relations

Table 9. List of those who can bring a claim before an industrial tribunal

All employees with a right to:
1 Fair dismissal or compensation for unfair dismissal.
2 Guarantee payments.
3 Medical suspension payments.
4 Protection against discrimination or victimisation because of activity in, or membership of, a trade union.
5 Time off for public duties.
6 Written reasons for dismissal.
7 Itemised pay statements.
8 Insolvency payments.
9 Redundancy consultation protective award.
10 Redundancy payments.
11 Paid time off to look for a job if redundant.
12 Interim relief if dismissed for trade union activities.
13 Protection against sex or marital discrimination.
14 Protection against racial discrimination.
15 Equal pay.
16 Written statement of terms of employment.

Women employees with a right to:
1 Protection from dismissal for pregnancy.
2 Suitable available alternative work during pregnancy.
3 Maternity pay.
4 Return to work following the birth of a child.
5 Paid time off for antenatal care.

Independent trade union officials/representatives/members with a right to:
1 Officials' paid time off for union duties and training.
2 Paid time off for safety representatives' training.
3 Representatives' right to redundancy consultation.
4 Members' right to membership, activity and time off.

Union members (or potential members) with a right to:
1 Protection against unreasonable exclusion or expulsion from a trade union when in employment where a union membership agreement applies.

it is felt that a principle is at stake, this can be costly in terms of time and money.

It is important if conciliation is chosen to make sure that the agreement is registered, through the Conciliation Officer, with the tribunal, to avoid subsequent difficulties.

84

The tribunal hearing

Each tribunal comprises a chairman (always an experienced lawyer) and two other members, one nominated by employer organisations and the other by employee organisations. They have the task of deciding whether the matter before them (eg the decision to dismiss) was 'reasonable in all the circumstances', taking into account the size and administrative resources of the employer.

Tribunals are run in a relatively informal way and have the ability to conduct proceedings in whatever manner they consider most suitable – avoiding formality and the strict rules governing admissibility of evidence applied in other courts. Individual employees are given every assistance to put their case especially if not legally represented. (Full legal aid is not available in tribunals and only about 35 per cent of employees are legally represented, though if they are trade union members, their union sometimes gives assistance.) It is not normal for a tribunal to award costs against either party, but they may do so if a case is brought or conducted frivolously, vexatiously or otherwise unreasonably.

Employers called before a tribunal to defend a case are also perfectly at liberty to act for themselves and there is much to be said for doing so – only the employer or manager knows the full circumstances of his organisation and its activities. It is likely to be wise, even so, to consult a legal adviser on the initial preparation of a case. Do not let the flexibility of tribunals lull you into a false sense of security. Seek advice, plan your case, prepare fully.

If necessary tribunals can request either party to take part in a pre-hearing assessment of the case that they intend to submit at the full hearing. If their case appears unlikely to succeed the tribunal will advise them of this, and that costs could be awarded if they choose to pursue their contentions to a full hearing.

Tribunals are open to the public, and it is worthwhile to visit the local tribunal to sit in on a few cases so as to see how they are handled, and the sort of information applicants and respondents are required to produce. This helps to learn about the importance of having good, well assembled written evidence to support the case, and of the usefulness of witnesses.

The HCITB's audio visual training aid *Reasonable in all the Circumstances?* gives more detail about industrial tribunals.

Statutory minimum notice periods

Under the Employment Protection (Consolidation) Act (Section 49) an employee working 16 hours per week or more (or eight hours per week after five years' service) is entitled to receive notice as follows:

(a) one week after one month's continuous service,
(b) two weeks after two years' continuous service,
(c) three weeks after three years' continuous service,
(d) to maximum 12 weeks after 12 years' continuous service.

The employee is required to give his employer one week's notice after one months' service.

These notice periods are the legal minima. Many employers give, and require to receive, *longer* periods of notice. This is perfectly acceptable, if agreed as part of the original contract.

There is an important exception: employees who have a contract for three months or less (eg seasonal workers) are not entitled to a week's notice unless they actually work for more than three months. This must be made clear at the time of engagement.

Sick employees

Employees who are sick for a lengthy period or for a series of short spells put an employer in a difficult situation. How long should they be kept on the books, with a job kept open, and when is it right to dismiss?

As in all dismissal cases, all the circumstances need to be examined. Particular attention should be paid to:

(a) The possibility of offering alternative employment.

(b) Ensuring that a full independent medical report is obtained, establishing when and if the employee will be able to return.

(c) Following the normal sickness scheme procedures.

(d) Ensuring consistency of treatment in different parts of the organisation and that length of service and circumstances etc, are taken into account.

(e) Making sure that the employee is given adequate warning before any final action such as dismissal is taken. If possible he should be visited, to establish his circumstances and to discuss the options available.

(f) In some circumstances, having found out as much as possible about the nature of the problem, an employer may be justified in giving a series of disciplinary warnings for short term sickness absences, which, if no improvement occurs could warrant dismissal on grounds of capability.

Fixed term contracts

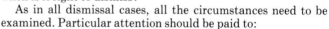

These are contracts of employment which end on a specific date and cannot normally be ended by either side giving notice before that date. The termination without renewal of such a contract can form the basis of a claim for unfair dismissal, unless the contract includes a waiver taking away the employee's right to claim unfair dismissal. The Employment Act 1980 (Section 8) enables fixed term contracts of one year or more to contain such a waiver clause (previously the contract had to be for two years or more).

17 Redundancy

P

If for some reason the workload of a business diminishes, it may be necessary to reduce staffing through redundancy. Sometimes this need can be avoided by introducing early retirement, or some form of work sharing. It is sensible to have an agreed policy stating how selection for redundancy will take place if it is necessary, and defining the payments to be made. The Department of Employment will give detailed guidance on entitlement to statutory redundancy payments which are based on age, length of service and weekly rate of pay.

L

Employees are entitled to compensation through the Redundancy Payments Scheme (RPS) so long as they are over the age of 18 and under the age of 65 (men), 60 (women) and have at least two years' continuous service over the age of 18. The employer makes these payments and claims back a percentage (at present 41 per cent) from the Department of Employment. It should be noted that:

(a) a payment must be claimed by an employee within six months of the date of termination of employment;

(b) unfair selection for redundancy enables the employee to claim unfair dismissal if he has the necessary qualifying period of continuous employment;

(c) it may constitute unlawful, indirect discrimination for part-time employees to be made redundant first; such action would have to be justified in a particular case, if unlawful discrimination was alleged.

Some employers negotiate redundancy payment schemes providing for payments to employees above the level required by the RPS.

Pre-consultation

Many organisations produce redundancy agreements as part of their normal employment practice, in which they specify the method of selection for redundancy, levels of payment etc. It has also always been regarded as being 'good industrial relations practice' to give as much notice as possible to employees to be made redundant, and the Employment Act 1980 reinforces this (as explained below).

The provisions apply to recognised independent trade unions and employees in most types of occupations. Unlike the redundancy payment provisions, they apply regardless of how long an employee has worked for his employer or for how many hours per week he is employed. The only exclusion important to our industry covers staff employed for a fixed term of three months or less (unless they are in fact employed beyond the third month).

Consulting the trade unions

An employer is required to consult appropriate trade unions about proposed redundancies so that, before individual re-dundancies are announced, the unions can discuss the plans to see whether there are ways of reducing the numbers involved or mitigating the effects of the redundancy.

If it is proposed to dismiss any employee as redundant and an independent trade union is recognised for the group or category of employees to which the redundant employee belongs, the employer must consult a representative of that trade union about the proposed dismissal at the earliest opportunity before it takes place. *The trade union must be consulted whether or not the employee is a member.*

The person consulted should be a representative of the union who is authorised by the union to carry on collective bargaining, for example the shop-steward, or the district union official, or, if appropriate, a national or regional official.

Consultation with the union concerned should always begin at the earliest opportunity, but if it is proposed to make ten or more employees redundant within a relatively short period, consultation must begin not later than a specified time before the first dismissal takes effect.

The minimum times are:

- if 10 to 99 employees may be dismissed as redundant at one establishment over a period of 30 days or less, *at least 30 days*
- if 100 or more employees may be dismissed as redundant at one establishment over a period of 90 days or less, *at least 90 days.*

An employer must give the trade union representatives details of the proposed redundancy, numbers and descriptions of those to be dismissed, proposed method of selection and dismissal. He must take note of, reply to and if possible adopt, any representations that are made about his proposals.

Even if circumstances change dramatically or with great speed he must take such steps to comply with the requirements as circumstances allow. If an employer fails to consult with the unions at the specified time, or take note of their proposals, or reply to them, the unions can apply to an industrial tribunal for a 'protective award' requiring the employer to continue to pay the employees concerned for a specified period.

The employer must also notify the Secretary of State for Employment of his proposal, through the regional Department of Employment office (see below).

No trade union involvement

Even if an employer does not recognise an independent trade union, he must still notify the Secretary of State for Employment (through the regional Department of Employment office) at least 30 days in advance if he proposes to make ten or more employees redundant at one establishment over a period of 30 days or less.

If 100 or more employees may be dismissed as redundant at one establishment within a period of 90 days or less, then notification must be given at least 90 days in advance. The purpose of this procedure is to allow the Employment Service Division of the MSC to plan to redeploy/retrain the staff involved.

Failure to carry out the notification may mean that the employer sacrifices up to one tenth of the rebate under the Redundancy Payments Scheme, or may be liable to a £400 fine on summary conviction.

The Department of Employment will need information in writing about the employer's plans in order to be able to carry out its functions. A notification form HR1 and a leaflet explaining the notification and consultation requirements can be obtained from any of its local offices or from the Employment Service Division of the MSC. The information required is similar to that which must be disclosed to trade unions for consultation.

Alternative employment trial period

A redundant employee is entitled to a four week trial period in any alternative employment the employer may offer him if the provisions of the new contract differ wholly or in part from the previous one. The trial period may be for longer than four weeks if both parties agree (but if so, the agreement must be in writing). For the purposes of the Redundancy Payments Act an extended trial period can be agreed, but only for training purposes.

The four week trial period is to enable both the employee and employer to decide whether the arrangement is satisfactory to both parties – if not, the redundancy payment entitlements are preserved and the claim for redundancy pay must be made within six months of the end of the trial period.

18 Employment rights on the transfer of an undertaking

The rights of employees working for a company which has been taken over or merged with another are specified in the Transfer of Undertakings (Protection of Employment) Regulations 1981, now in force.

Under the Regulations, employees who are employed by the old employer at the time of transfer, automatically become the employees of the new employer, as if their contracts of employment were originally made with the new employer. The new employer takes over the employment liabilities of the old employer, with the exception of criminal liabilities and occupational pension rights.

If there is an independent trade union recognised for the purpose of collective bargaining, the trade union representatives of the employees affected have to be informed about the transfer, and also, if the old or the new employer intends taking measures in relation to the transfer affecting the employees, have to be consulted about the proposed measures.

ACAS will advise if there is any doubt – for example as to whether a particular transfer is covered by the Regulations.

Any dismissal of an employee for a reason connected with the transfer will be considered unfair unless it can be shown that the dismissal was necessary for an economic, technical or organisational reason and that the employer acted reasonably in dismissing for such a reason. In such cases redundancy provisions may apply and further advice may be obtained from the nearest Jobcentre, unemployment benefit office or Redundancy Payments Office.

19 Working conditions

Employers have a duty under the Health and Safety at Work, etc, Act 1974 to ensure the health, safety and welfare of all their employees. Employers must prepare a written statement of their general policy (where five or more are employed) and bring it to the notice of their employees. In addition to the minimum standards required, as appropriate, by the law (see below), it is worth providing conditions that are as pleasant as possible, to improve staff morale and increase productivity.

Specific requirements covering working conditions are included in a number of Acts, for example the Factories Act 1961 and the Offices, Shops and Railway Premises Act 1963. In addition, food hygiene and other regulations specify minimum acceptable standards for work practices concerning the preparation, storage and serving of food.

For further detailed guidance contact the local office of the Health and Safety Executive, or your local Environmental Health Officer. The basic working conditions dealt with by the law cover:

- space – a minimum of 400 cubic feet per employee
- temperature
- washing and sanitary facilities
- drinking water
- ventilation and lighting
- facilities for the storage of clothing
- sitting facilities
- plant and machinery (especially the provision and use of lifts and guards)
- safe passage ways, entrances and exits
- safe handrails, floor surfaces and fencing
- adequate fire emergency facilities.

The HCITB book *Training for Health and Safety* gives more information on a number of these matters.

20 First aid regulations

The Health and Safety (First Aid) Regulations 1981 require all places of employment, except domestic service, to be provided with adequate first aid facilities. The Regulations, which are explained in more detail in the code of practice available from HMSO, require that:

(a) employers must provide first aid equipment, facilities, and personnel adequate and appropriate to the circumstances of the employer (see below);

(b) an employer must inform his employees of the arrangements (a health and safety policy statement could be an appropriate means);

(c) self-employed persons are required 'to provide adequate equipment to enable first aid to be rendered to themselves'.

In some circumstances it is necessary for the employer to ensure that there are suitably trained and qualified people to render first aid to employees. Where a trained first aider is not a requirement, a person must be appointed to take charge of situations involving injury or illness, and the first aid equipment and facilities. More than one person may be needed to ensure cover at all times that employees are on the premises. Those appointed will need training in, for example, the action to take in the event of an accident, the maintenance of first aid equipment and reporting procedures.

The Health and Safety Executive publication *First Aid at Work* gives guidelines on when it is necessary to have a trained first aider; briefly it depends on:
- the number of employees
- the nature of the undertaking
- the degree of hazard in the work
- the size of the establishment and distribution of the employees.

21 Employee relations training

In this book employment practices have been suggested which are likely to establish sound employee relations within the context of the legislation.

Reviewing existing practices

From time to time, organisations should review their employment practices and employee relations policy to establish where improvements can be made. This should not only be done with employment legislation in mind but with a view to better understanding between management and staff.

Carrying out such a review may highlight:

• need for changes in the organisation

• need for changes in procedures or for the development of clear policies

• areas where costs need to be reduced or standards improved

• areas where gaps in knowledge and skill need to be filled by appropriate training.

Many organisations have adopted the practice of carrying out a periodic 'audit' of their employee relations policies and practices. ACAS will carry out such work free of charge. Such an audit might include:

• interviews or attitude surveys with managers, staff and their representatives

• an examination of procedures, rules and records in the light of legal requirements and current 'good practice'.

Audits are used to identify the cause of current problems and as a means of problem prevention. They also yield valuable information about training needs and are useful in that they give factual information and do not rely on subjective opinion. (Further details are given in *Analysing Industrial Relations,* a guide published by Employment Relations Ltd.)

Training needs

Employee relations is essentially practical, concerned with the ways in which people at work interact in their work situation. *Skills* and *attitudes* are just as important as *knowledge* and *information.* So when training plans are being made they may need to include how to improve levels of skill in such activities as:

• negotiation

• interviewing (eg discipline, counselling or selection of staff)

- understanding employees' motivation and attitudes
- communicating – verbally or in writing
- conduct of meetings (as chairman or committee member)
- social and interpersonal skills.

Employee relations training should be tackled systematically. In this aspect it is no different from other training; indeed employee relations training should form part of the company's overall training plan. The HCITB's companion titles *A Guide to Systematic Training* and *Training Your Staff* set out how to go about training in a systematic way.

One of the aims of this book is to enable employers to identify not only what their legal requirements are in respect of employee relations, but what good practices should be considered. Checklist 5 provides further suggestions to help establish training needs, but it is also important for the policy maker of a business to have a wide and up to date knowledge of the subject, to be aware of what is happening in employee relations in the industry and the country generally, what other employers are doing locally (not just in the hotel and catering industry) and what trade union and Government attitudes and plans are.

Checklist 5

Training needs analysis

Are personnel policy makers aware of:

1. Trends in legislation?
2. Trade union activity in the industry and in general?
3. The role of trade or other advisory bodies?
4. The effect of employee relations policy on day-to-day practice?

Are those implementing employee relations policy aware of:

1. The effect of policy on day-to-day practice?
2. Their role in implementing the policy?

Does the company's recruitment/selection policy/procedure conform with good employee relations practice:

1. Describing the job?
2. Describing the person?
3. Advertising?
4. Interviewing techniques?
5. Sex discrimination?
6. Race discrimination?
7. Work permits?

8 Employing disabled people?

9 Employing ex-offenders?

10 Use of references?

11 Are key company personnel aware of the requirements of the law and good employee relations practice regarding recruitment/selection:

    (a) the policy makers?

    (b) managers?

    (c) supervisors?

    (d) staff representatives?

Does the company's engagement/administration policy/procedure conform with good employee relations practice:

1 Induction?

2 Written statement of terms of employment?

3 Company pay policy?

4 Company pay procedures?

5 Wages council orders?

6 Equal pay?

7 Hours of work?

8 Shift arrangements?

9 Training policy?

10 Health and safety policy?

11 Staff records?

12 Staff appraisal?

13 Are key company personnel aware of the requirements of the law and good employee relations practice regarding engagement of staff and administration policy/procedures:

    (a) the policy makers?

    (b) managers?

    (c) supervisors?

    (d) staff representatives?

14 Are all employees aware of those aspects of the company's administration policy that affect them?

Does the company's leave and absence arrangements conform with good employee relations practice, with regard to time off for:

1 Union official duties?

2 Union activity?

3 Public duties?

4 Redundant employees?

5 Sickness?

6 Holidays?

7 Pregnancy?

8 Payment for time off?

9 Are key company personnel aware of the requirements of the law and good employee relations practice regarding leave and absence arrangements:

(a) the policy makers?
(b) managers?
(c) supervisors?
(d) staff representatives?

10 Are all employees aware of the company's leave and absence arrangements?

If the company recognises a trade union:

1 Do its arrangements for joint consultation and other matters conform with good employee relations practice?

2 Are key company personnel aware of the structure of the union?

3 Is the role of shop stewards/staff representatives clear?

4 Are key personnel trained in negotiating skills?

5 Are key personnel aware of the role of procedure and other agreements with the trade union?

6 Are key personnel aware of what information should go to:

(a) union members?
(b) union representatives?
(c) non-union members?

Are company personnel at all levels aware of:

1 The role and purpose of staff committees/associations?

2 The role of staff representatives?

3 The role of safety representatives?

Does the company's grievance and disciplinary procedure conform with good employee relations practice:

1 Policies?

2 Company rules?

3 Procedures?

4 Warnings/appeals/time limits?

5 Representation?

6 Fair dismissal?

7 Constructive dismissal?

8 Instant dismissal?

9 Suspension?

10 Unfair dismissal?

11 Wrongful dismissal?

12 Who can claim unfair dismissal?

13 Redundancy?

14 Retirement?

15 Are company personnel aware of the requirements of the law and good employee relations practice regarding grievance and disciplinary procedures:
   (a) the policy makers?
   (b) managers?
   (c) supervisors?
   (d) staff representatives?

Planning and carrying out the training

Basic information and explanations should be given as part of an employee's induction. For example, explanation of company policies and procedures, information about their conditions and terms of employment and ensuring that disciplinary rules are understood.

Where changes are taking place it may be necessary to consider special training programmes. For example, if a negotiating agreement is reached with a trade union, extensive training for supervisors and managers will be needed in:
- matters covered by the agreement
- the role of the staff representative
- rights to time off for trade union matters.

Supervisors and managers may need special assistance in dealing with staff representatives for the first time.

There are a number of different types of programme that can be devised, depending on a company's needs and circumstances. These are given in Table 10.

There is no one best way of carrying out employee relations training. Suitable arrangements need to be made taking into account the needs and circumstances of the organisation.

Deciding on the most appropriate training methods to meet a company's needs and objectives will not be an easy task. The HCITB will help either directly through an employer's local training adviser, or by giving information on specific training methods and aids, and specialist help is available in particular subject areas.

Each region of the Board has specialists with a particular interest and expertise in employee relations training. They will be pleased to help and advise (addresses in Appendix VI).

Employee Relations

Table 10
Employee
relations
training
programmes

---

1 Basic training

. . . training associated with setting up a basic employee relations framework. This means identifying the specific functions, roles and jobs of those involved in the employee relations process and providing training in appropriate skills and knowledge. This will be individual training for each person and group involved to establish a sound basis on which further training can be built. This first level training can then lead on to . . .

2 Updating training

. . . training to support an established framework by strengthening basic skills and knowledge or developing new ones. Updating training will involve continuous monitoring and be related to specific changes (often minor) arising from, for example, actual or planned changes in employee relations policy, legislation, environment and circumstances. This training might then need to be supplemented by . . .

3 Training for major change

. . . training related to major change which demands detailed and comprehensive plans to be made. The changes are likely to be specific and have a potentially high impact on the employee relations system, eg recognition of other unions, productivity agreements, job evaluation schemes, legislation. This is a key area for trainers in terms of current development at national level and the whole social and economic environment in which companies have to operate. Finally, consideration might be given to . . .

4 Training for the future

. . . training to develop a favourable employee relations environment or climate in the longer term. This training is likely to be of a less specific nature. Its objective, for example, might be to:

- promote a climate within which employee relations can develop on a continuing basis
- build a joint working approach to identifying and solving problems
- develop a maturity of approach and relationships, leading to greater joint involvement in the operation of the business.

Appendix I
Glossary of terms

Arbitration
A process by which parties involved in a dispute over which they have been unable to reach an agreement agree to submit to the decision of an independent judge. It is usually agreed, in advance, to accept the decision as binding.

Associated employer
Any two employers are associated if one is a company of which another (directly or indirectly) has control, or if both are companies of which a third person (directly or indirectly) has control.

Casual worker
As defined by the LRE&LR wages council, this is 'a person who cannot be required to work if he has not on each occasion previously undertaken to do so'.

Certification Officer
Official responsible for giving certificates of independence to trade unions, checking union accounts, and dealing with financial assistance for union ballots.

Check-off
Direct deduction of union dues from wages by the employer (who then pays the dues to the union). A small percentage is sometimes retained by the employer to cover his administrative costs.

Closed shop
An agreement to set up a closed shop is referred to as a *union membership agreement* (UMA) in employment legislation (TULRA, EA80). There are two main types of closed shop:
(a) pre-entry: individuals are excluded from work unless they are already members of a specified union to which the other workers belong;

(b) post entry: new employees are required to join the union within an agreed period of starting work.

Code of practice
A document produced by an official body (eg ACAS) which gives guidance on an employment matter although it can be cited in legal proceedings. A person cannot be prosecuted for failing to observe any of its provisions.

Collective agreement
Any agreement or arrangement made by or on behalf of one or more trade unions and one or more employers or employers' associations and relating to one or more of the matters listed below under *collective bargaining*. That is, employers do not negotiate individually, but collectively through representatives.

Collective bargaining
Negotiations intended to result in a collective agreement governing the relationship between the parties involved in the following matters:
(a) terms and conditions of employment, or the physical conditions in which any workers are required to work;
(b) engagement or non-engagement, or termination or suspension of employment, or the duties of employment of one or more workers;
(c) allocation of work or the duties of employment as between workers or groups of workers;
(d) matters of discipline;
(e) the membership or non-membership of a trade union on the part of a worker;
(f) facilities for officials of trade unions;
(g) machinery for negotiation or consultation, and other procedures relating to any of the foregoing matters, including the recognition by employers or

employers' associations of the right of a trade union to represent workers in any such negotiation or consultation or in the carrying out of such procedures.

Conciliation

Process by which the opposing parties in a dispute are brought together and helped by an outside party to resolve the dispute – can occur *individually* (as in unfair dismissal cases) or *collectively* (larger industrial disputes). If collective conciliation fails then the final stage of the process is often to attempt to obtain agreement to and terms of reference for *arbitration (qv)* on the matter.

Continuity of employment

Many employment rights can only be claimed after an employee has been employed continuously for a specified period. Thus it is often important to be able to clarify whether a particular period of employment is continuous, or whether breaks such as maternity leave, sickness, or short time working have broken the continuity.

In any proceedings under employee's rights legislation, the employee's period of employment is presumed to have been continuous unless the employer proves otherwise. Disputes are dealt with by industrial tribunals.

Basically, to count towards a continuous period of employment, a work week must be one in which:

(a) the employee is actually employed for 16 hours or more; or

(b) the contract with the employer to work 16 hours or more continues, even if 16 hours are not worked (eg because of holidays, sickness); or

(c) the employee, having been employed for five years, works under a contract for eight hours or more a week.

For further details (this is a complex issue) see Department of Employment booklet No 11.

Craft union

The oldest form of trade union in which members are engaged in the same skilled occupation or craft. One of the aims of such a union may be to regulate entry to the particular occupation, in an attempt to protect jobs.

Custom and practice

Refers to activities which may not be formally agreed between management and staff but which have come to be accepted as normal by continual practice.

Employee relations

See *Industrial relations* below.

Employers' association

Organisation of employers whose principal purposes include regulations of relations between employers and workers (eg Engineering Employers' Federation but not trade associations such as the Brewers' Society and the BHRCA).

General unions

Large, national trade unions having as members workers from a very wide range of industries. Members can be unskilled, semi-skilled or skilled, such unions (eg TGWU) also have separate sections for supervisory members.

Genuine occupational qualification (GOQ)

A term used to describe a situation in which the requirements of a job are such that only a member of a particular sex or race can effectively carry the job out, for example being of a particular racial group can be a GOQ for some acting; being a model, or working as a waiter in an ethnic restaurant. Such GOQ's are not automatic exceptions to the law on discrimination; each case needs to be taken on its merits.

Independent trade union

A trade union which is not under the domination or control of an employer or a group of employers or of one or more employers' associations, and is not liable to interference by an employer or any such group or association (arising out of the provision of financial or material support or by any other means whatsoever) tending towards such control.

Note only independent trade unions qualify for the benefits contained in TULRA, EPA and EA80. Unions have to apply to the Certification Officer to obtain conclusive evidence of independence.

Industrial relations

Defined as 'the practice, or the study, of relationships within and between workers, working groups and their organisations and managers, employers and their organisations', Marsh, *Concise Encyclopaedia of Industrial Relations*. A simpler definition has been used elsewhere: 'All the issues involved in the reward – work equation'.

Job evaluation

A term used to cover a number of systematic methods of determining the relative worth of jobs in a manner acceptable to the job holders.

Joint consultation

The process by which employers and employees discuss, before any decisions are taken, matters affecting the efficiency of the enterprise and the interests of the employees to which representatives can contribute. It is generally carried out by committees, incorporating trade union representatives if applicable, with an agreed constitution.

Joint regulation

A term used to refer to arrangements allowing both staff and management to participate in the management and development of the organisation.

Mediation

The process of attempting to reach an agreement with the help of an independent third party, who makes recommendations which are not binding, but may provide a means of settling a previously insoluble problem.

Negotiation

Bargaining carried out between two parties, generally over terms and conditions of employment, such as pay and hours.

Procedure agreement

An agreement made between an employer or employers' association and trade union(s) describing the machinery to be used for consultation, or settlement by negotiation, of terms and conditions of employment, including trade union recognition, facilities for shop-stewards, dismissal, redundancy, grievances, etc.

Thus a procedure agreement defines how, at what level, problems arising, and settlement of *substantive agreements (qv)* can be dealt with.

Recognition

The process by which an employer agrees to deal with a union representing all or some of his staff. The terms of recognition are usually set out in a *recognition agreement*. Often, recognition starts with an agreement that the employer will deal with the union on disciplinary matters only. The scope of the agreement may then be gradually widened by mutual agreement, until it relates to all of the matters referred to in the definition of *collective bargaining (qv)*.

Recognition agreement

The written statement describing recognition arrangements between an employer and union. Though recognition is not always formalised in writing it is sensible to avoid confusion by producing a written agreement setting out the degree of recognition granted.

Reinstatement

In the context of Section 69 of the EP(C)A this term refers to an order made against an employer by an industrial tribunal requiring that an employee be reinstated in his job and that he be treated in all respects (seniority, pension rights, pay etc) as if he had not been dismissed.

Shop steward/staff representative

A member of the trade union who is elected by union members in the department or section he represents, in elections held according to union rules. He represents the views and interests of his colleagues, and is a vehicle for communicating management proposals to them. The senior shop-steward is sometimes referred to as the *convenor*.

Staff association/house union

An organisation established, and often financed, by an employer to facilitate communication and consultation with his staff.

Understandably, staff associations are not popular with the independent trade unions. Because of this, and because of the unavoidable influence of the employer, staff associations may be unstable and can be ineffective in a situation of conflict.

Status quo

An arrangement whereby, if a particular change, eg of working arrangements, causes a dispute, it is agreed to revert to the original practice until agreement is reached.

Statutory Joint Industrial Council (SJIC)

An SJIC is a body, similar to the wages council, which has the power to set minimum terms and conditions of employment for an industry. It differs from a wages council in being able to appoint its own members and, having no independent members, is intended as a halfway house between wages councils and full collective bargaining. The idea has, in reality, made little progress.

Substantive agreement

This type of agreement between a trade union and employer sets out the terms of employment which it has jointly been decided will apply. It can deal with matters such as wages and other payments, hours of work, overtime, holidays, grading, manpower planning, pensions, redundancy and other matters affecting work organisation. Some substantive agreements will be restricted to a few of these items. The machinery used for arriving at a substantive agreement is described in a *procedure agreement (qv)*.

Trade dispute

A dispute between workers and their employer connected wholly or mainly with any of the following matters:

(a) terms and conditions of employment, or the physical conditions in which any workers are required to work;

(b) engagement or non-engagement, or termination or suspension of employment or the duties of employment, of one or more workers;

(c) allocation of work or the duties of employment as between workers or groups of workers;

(d) matters of discipline;

(e) the membership or non-membership of a trade union on the part of a worker;

(f) facilities for officials of trade unions; and

(g) machinery for negotiation or consultation, and other procedures, relating to any of the foregoing matters, including the recognition by employers or employers' associations of the right of a trade union to represent workers in any such negotiation or consultation or in the carrying out of such procedures.

Trade union

An organisation of workers whose principal purposes include the regulation of relations between workers and employers. A union on the Certification Officers' list gets tax relief, and can apply to be categorised as *independent (qv)*.

Trade union recognition

The recognition of the union by an employer, or two or more associated employers, to any extent, for the purpose of *collective bargaining (qv)*.

Union membership agreement

See *closed shop*.

Union official

Any person who is an officer of the union, or of a branch or section of the union or who (not being such an officer) is a person elected or appointed in accordance with the rules of the union to be a representative of its members or some of them, including any person so elected or appointed who is an employee of the same employer as the members, or one or more of the members, whom he is to represent.

Week

As defined in EP(C)A, a *week* means, in relation to an employee whose remuneration is calculated weekly ending with a day other than Saturday, a week ending with that other day, and in relation to any other employee, a week ending with Saturday.

White collar unions

Term used to describe unions representing the interests of clerical, administrative, technical and management staff (eg ASTMS, APEX and, in our industry, NALHM). Some large general unions also have white collar sections (eg MATSA in the GMBATU and ACTS in TGWU).

Appendix II

Where to obtain further help

ORGANISATION	ASSISTANCE AVAILABLE
Advisory, Conciliation and Arbitration Service (ACAS) 11/12 St James's Square London SW1 Tel: 01-214 6000 Requests for advice can also be made to ACAS regional offices (see local telephone directory)	Free advice and practical assistance on employee relations problems. Codes of practice and advisory booklets on personnel records, payment systems, job evaluation, and other matters. Conciliation and arbitration services on a variety of matters.
The Brewers' Society 42 Portman Square London W1H 0BB Tel: 01-486 4831	Information and guidance service for members.
British Association for Commercial and Industrial Education (BACIE) 16 Park Crescent London W1N 4AP Tel: 01-636 5351	Wide range of publications, courses and seminars.
British Hotels Restaurants and Caterers Association (BHRCA) 40 Duke Street London W1M 6HR Tel: 01-499 6641	Information and advice service for members. Various publications including *Guide to Main Provisions of Licensed Residential Establishment Wages Council.*
British Institute of Innkeeping 42 Portman Square London W1H 0BB Tel: 01-486 4831	Information and advice service for members. Seminars.
British Institute of Management (BIM) Management House Parker Street London WC2B 5PT Tel: 01-405 3456	Information and advice service for members. Books and seminars. Management checklist on a variety of industrial relations topics.

Employee Relations

ORGANISATION	ASSISTANCE AVAILABLE
Central Office of Industrial Tribunals: *England and Wales:* 93 Ebury Bridge Road London SW1W 8RE Tel: 01-730 9161	Information on industrial tribunal operation and procedures.
Scotland: St Andrew House 141 West Nile Street Glasgow G1 2RU Tel: 041-331 1601	
Commission for Racial Equality (CRE) Elliott House 10–12 Allington Street London SW1E 5EH Tel: 01-828 7022	Information and advice on employment matters relating to race and nationality, including a *Race Relations Code of Practice,* and papers on *Equal Opportunity in Employment, Monitoring an Equal Opportunity Policy* and *Why Keep Ethnic Records?*
Department of Employment Caxton House Tothill Street London SW1H 9NA Tel: 01-213 3000 Regional offices in Birmingham, Bristol, Cardiff, Edinburgh, Leeds, London, Manchester and Newcastle upon Tyne	Wide range of publications (see Appendix III). Advice on local labour market/recruitment services (via Jobcentres and Professional and Executive Register).
Employment Relations Limited 62–64 Hills Road Cambridge Tel: (0223) 315944	Reference library of industrial relations training material, register of trainers and consultants and limited advisory service. Also produces a range of training materials, packages etc.
Equal Opportunities Commission (EOC) Overseas House Quay Street Manchester M3 3HN Tel: 061-833 9244	Advice on Sex Discrimination Act and Equal Pay Act. Assistance in the development of equal opportunities policies, and job evaluation free of sex bias. Range of publications (see Appendix III).

ORGANISATION   ASSISTANCE AVAILABLE

The trade unions principally involved in the industry and who may be able to assist, are:

General Municipal Boilermakers and Allied Trades Union
Thorne House, Ruxley Ridge
Claygate, Esher, Surrey KT10 0TL

Tel: (78) 62081

Hotel and Catering Workers' Union
Thorne House, Ruxley Ridge
Claygate, Esher, Surrey KT10 0TL

Tel: (78) 62081

National Association of Licensed House Managers
9 Coombe Lane
London SW20 8NE

Tel: 01-947 3080

National Union of Railwaymen
Unity House
Euston Road
London NW1 2BL

Tel: 01-387 4771

Transport and General Workers' Union
Transport House, Smith Square
London SW1P 3JB

Tel: 01-828 7788

Transport Salaried Staffs' Association
Walkden House, Melton Street
London NW1 2EJ

Tel: 01-387 2101

Union of Shop, Distributive and Allied Workers
Oakley, 188 Wilmslow Road
Fallowfield, Manchester M14 6LJ

Tel: 061-224 2804

Hotel and Catering Industry Training Board (HCITB)
PO Box 18, Ramsey House
Central Square, Wembley
Middlesex HA9 7AP

Tel: 01-902 8865

Regional offices in Altrincham, Bristol, Eastbourne, Edinburgh and York (addresses in Appendix VI) and an area office in Newmarket.

Books, training aids, audio visual material, seminars and courses, information and advice on training in employee relations. Material available includes:

- *Getting a Good Deal,* a manual for training in negotiating and the development of influencing skills, with OHP viewfoils

- *Employing People in the Licensed Trade,* a self-help guide

- *'Qué'?* how to identify communication training needs in the multi-racial workplace

- *Reasonable in all the Circumstances?* a training package containing a video tape simulating an industrial tribunal and a tutor's manual.

Employee Relations

ORGANISATION	ASSISTANCE AVAILABLE
Hotel, Catering and Institutional Management Association (HCIMA) 191 Trinity Road London SW17 7HN Tel: 01-672 4251	Information service for members. Wide range of directories and reading lists. Monthly magazine *Hospitality* and twice monthly *HCIMA News and Appointments.* Conditions of employment advice for members.
Hotel and Catering Personnel and Training Association Membership Secretary: Pat Primarolo 1 Springhill Cottages Shipbourne Nr Sevenoaks, Kent Tel: (0732) 810602	An association of specialists from the industry who offer advice and regular meetings with the chance to discuss matters of mutual interest and concern.
The Industrial Society Peter Runge House 3 Carlton House Terrace London SW1 Tel: 01-839 4300	In-company advice and training on management and industrial relations. Job evaluation exercises undertaken. Publications, information and conferences. Consultancy services also available.
Institute of Personnel Management (IPM) IPM House 35 Camp Road Wimbledon London SW19 4UW Tel: 01-946 9100	Wide range of publications and courses. Special 'Company Service Plan' for small firms with no professional personnel department.
Local colleges and Regional Management Centres (See local telephone directory or consult your HCITB Adviser)	Various colleges specialise in personnel/industrial relations and run courses or will advise on particular topics.
Local Government Training Board 4th Floor, Arndale House Arndale Centre Luton LU1 2TS Tel: (0582) 21111	Courses, publications, training advice.

ORGANISATION	ASSISTANCE AVAILABLE
National Centre of Industrial Language Training (NCILT) Havelock Campus Havelock Road Southall Middlesex UB2 4NZ Tel: 01-571 2241	Information and assistance in training ethnic minority workers in the use of English, and to inform employers about the communications training needs of such employees and their managers. The ILT Services and HCITB have jointly published a guide on the subject '*Qué*'?, the analysis of communications training needs in the multi-racial workplace.
Office of Wages Councils Steel House London SW1H 9NF	For copies of current Wages Council Orders (LR or LNR).
Open University Associate Student Central Office PO Box 76 Milton Keynes MK7 6AN Tel: (0908) 653003	Post experience course in industrial relations, incorporating case study *Room for Reform?* on the hotel industry.
Small Firms Information Centres To contact your Regional Centre, dial 100 and ask the operator for National Freefone 2444.	Advice on problems relating to small businesses.

Appendix III
Training aids and booklets

Advisory, Conciliation and Arbitration Service

ACAS has produced the following advisory booklets: No 1, *Job Evaluation*, No 2, *Introduction to Payment Systems*, No 3, *Personnel Records*, No 4, *Labour Turnover*, No 5, *Absence*, No 6, *Recruitment and Selection*, No 7, *Induction of New Employees*, No 8, *Workplace Communications*, and No 9, *The Company Handbook*. These are available free of charge from ACAS (address in Appendix II). Future advisory booklets in this series are planned.

The following are available free of charge:
- *This is ACAS*
- *Advice on Personnel Management and Industrial Relations Practice*
- *Assistance with Industrial Relations Problems*
- *Conciliation, Arbitration, Mediation in Trade Disputes*
- *Improving Industrial Relations – A Joint Responsibility*
- *Conciliation between Individuals and their Employers.*

Other ACAS publications include:
- Report No 18 *Licensed Residential Establishment and Licensed Restaurant Wages Council* (which gives a useful account of industrial relations in this sector of the industry – out-of-print, but possibly available from local libraries)
- *Industrial Relations Handbook* (a comprehensive guide to British industrial relations, available from HMSO)
- *Code of Practice No 1: Disciplinary Practice and Procedures in Employment* (reproduced in Appendix IV)
- *Code of Practice No 2: Disclosure of Information to Trade Unions for Collective Bargaining Purposes*
- *Code of Practice No 3: Time off for Trade Union Duties and Activities.*

BBC Enterprises

Many of the interesting *Man at Work* programmes and other TV documentaries can be hired as films or videotapes from the BBC, often with supporting literature. Examples include *Representing the Union, People Ltd, Member of the Union* and *Unfair Dismissal*.

Details from BBC Enterprises, Film Hire, Woodston House, Oundle Road, Peterborough PE2 9PZ, tel: (0733) 52257/8.

Croner Publications Ltd

Croner Publications produce a number of reference books (loose-leaf in a ring binder), updated regularly, including:
- *Croner's Reference Book for Employers*
- *Croner's Employment Law*
- *Catering* (which includes a section on employment).

Details from Croner Publications Ltd, Croner House, 173 Kingston Road, New Malden, Surrey KT3 3SS, tel: 01-942 8966.

Department of Employment

Employment Gazette, published monthly, contains statistics on employment and up-to-date information on changes in legislation. It can be consulted at most public reference libraries or obtained on subscription from HMSO.

The Department of Employment and Employment Division of the MSC also produce a range of guides to employment legislation. These guides, together with a comprehensive 192 page students' edition, can be obtained, normally free of charge, from Department of Employment and ED offices. Other titles include:
- *Employment News* (the Department of Employment newspaper)
- *Employing Disabled People*
- *The Truck Acts*
- *Employment of Foreign Nationals in Great Britain*
- *Employment of Overseas Workers in Great Britain*
- *Codes of Practice on Picketing and the Closed Shop.*

Employment Relations Ltd

As part of their role as the national resource centre for industrial relations training, Employment Relations Ltd publish a range of training publications and packages. Examples include:
- Multi-media programmes including *Grievance Handling, An Introduction to Negotiation, Discord, Collective Bargaining*
- Publications for the trainer and industrial relations specialist including *Industrial Relations and the Supervisor, Analysing Industrial Relations, Factfile 3: Employment Law,* and *Discipline*
- Training material for the Youth Training Scheme.

Further information from Employment Relations Ltd, 62 Hills Road, Cambridge CB2 1LA, tel: (0223) 315944.

Equal Opportunities Commission

The EOC produces a wide range of booklets and guides on all aspects of sex discrimination and equal pay including *A Model Equal Opportunity Policy, Equality at Work,* and *So you think you've got it right.* A list of publications and visual aids is available from the EOC (address in Appendix II).

Gower TFI Ltd

Gower TFI (in 1983 Gower Publishing took over Training Films International) publish a range of useful publications, including the *Concise Encyclopaedia of Industrial Relations* by Arthur E

Marsh and, by the same author, *Trade Union Handbook: A Guide and Directory of the Structure, Membership, Policy and Personnel of British Trade Unions* (2nd edition).

The company also distributes a wide range of films.

Details from Gower TFI, Gower House, Croft Road, Aldershot, Hants GU11 3HR, tel: (0252) 331551.

Guild Training

A wide range of training programmes are available from Guild Training, a division of The Guild Organisation, including management training, sales training, hygiene and safety in catering. Catalogues are available from Guild Training, Guild House, Peterborough PE2 9PZ, tel: (0733) 52255.

Home Office

The following Home Office guides are published by HMSO:

● *Racial Discrimination – a Guide to the Race Relations Act 1976*

● *Sex Discrimination – a Guide to the Sex Discrimination Act 1975*

● *A Guide to the Rehabilitation of Offenders Act 1974*

HM Stationery Office

HMSO stock the relevant Acts of Parliament and a range of other industrial relations and training publications, listed in *Sectional List 21 – Department of Employment.*

Codes of practice, produced by ACAS, are available from HMSO, as is the code of practice *The First Aid Regulations.*

HMSO address for mail order is 51 Nine Elms Lane, London SW8 5DR, telephone enquiries 01-211 8661.

Incomes Data Services Ltd

An independent research centre reporting on all aspects of industrial relations. IDS publishes fortnightly reports on pay changes, studies of pay and other conditions of groups of workers, the decisions of industrial tribunals, and changes to pay and conditions in EEC countries. Among other publications is a monthly review of management pay.

Details from Incomes Data Services, 140 Portland Street, London W1, tel: 01-580 0521.

Institute of Personnel Management

IPM produce a wide range of publications on employment subjects (over 120 titles are now listed). A catalogue is available from the Publications Sales Department of the Institute (address in Appendix II).

Industrial Relations Briefing

Publishers of a range of guidebooks and reference texts on employee relations and health and safety matters. Titles include:

● *Trade Unions – Law and Practice*

● *Employment Act 1980*

● Question and answer booklets on a variety of topics

● *Health and Safety – the Law.*

Details from IRB, Book Sales Division, 346 Harrow Road, London W9 2HP, tel: 01-289 1158.

Industrial Relations Services

IRS publish *Industrial Relations Review and Report,* a twice monthly publication which summarises and comments on significant industrial relations matters and tribunal and EAT cases. Also available from IRS are:
- *Pay and Benefits Bulletin*
- *Industrial Relations Legal Information Bulletin*
- *Health and Safety Information Bulletin*
- *Industrial Relations Law Reports.*

Details from Industrial Relations Services, 67 Maygrove Road, London NW6 2EJ, tel: 01-328 4751.

Industrial Society

The Industrial Society publishes a wide range of booklets and training programmes, including:
- booklets on a range of management topics in the series *Notes for Managers* (including communications/industrial relations/joint consultation/employment practices)
- guides to various pieces of employment legislation
- audio visual presentations.

A catalogue of publications is available from Industrial Society (address in Appendix II).

Kogan Page Ltd

Kogan Page publish a range of books including:
- *Industrial Relations Training for Managers* by Chris Brewster and Stephen Connock (1981)
- *Personnel and Training Management Yearbook and Directory*
- *An A-Z of Employment and Safety Law* by Peter Chandler (1981).

Details from Kogan Page Ltd, 120 Pentonville Road, London N1 9JN, tel: 01-837 7851.

Low Pay Unit and Counter Information Services

These two pressure groups are based at 9 Poland Street, London W1V 3DG. They have published a number of controversial reports on pay, conditions and wages councils, including one, *Hardship Hotel,* specifically on the hotel and catering industry.

National Economic Development Office

Whilst in existence the Hotels and Catering EDC produced a number of reports including the following:
- *Your Manpower. A Practical Guide to the Manpower Statistics of the Hotel and Catering Industry,* HMSO, London 1967
- *Service in Hotels,* HMSO, London 1968
- *Staff Turnover,* HMSO, London 1969
- *Why Tipping?* HMSO, London 1969
- *Manpower Policy in the Hotels and Restaurant Industry: Research Findings Summary and Recommendations,* 2 Vols, NEDO, London 1975

● *Employment Policy and Industrial Relations in the Hotel and Catering Industry,* NEDO, London 1977.

These are now out of print, but may be available through a good reference library.

Rank Aldis Films A number of training films are available from Rank Aldis for hire or purchase. Topics range from discipline interviewing, communication and induction to industrial safety and styles of leadership. Many of the films are British made. Details from Rank Audio Visual Ltd, PO Box 70, Great West Road, Brentford, Middlesex; for film hire bookings, tel: 01-568 9222.

Trades Union Congress The TUC produces a number of useful publications such as:
● *British Trade Unions* (an introduction for newcomers to this country)
● *Facilities for Shop Stewards*
● *TUC Guides* (guidelines on negotiating procedures, conduct of disputes and union organisation)
● *Safety and Health at Work*
● *Law of Trusts and Pension Schemes.*

Details of these are obtainable from the Publications Department, TUC, Congress House, Great Russell Street, London WC1B 3LS, tel: 01-636 4030.

Other publications ● Bain, G S (ed), *Industrial Relations in Britain,* Blackwell, 1983
● Bell, John, *An Employee Management Handbook,* Engineering Industry Training Board and Stanley Thornes (Publishers) Ltd, 1981 (a practical guide on managing people and employment law)
● Boella, M J, *Personnel Management· in the Hotel and Catering Industry,* 3rd edition, Hutchinson, London 1983
● Bull, F J, Hooper, J D G, *Hotel and Catering Law. An Outline of the Law Relating to Hotels, Guest Houses, Restaurants and Other Catering Businesses,* 7th edition, Barrie and Jenkins, London 1979
● Chandler, P A, *The Hotel and Catering Manager's Guide to the Law,* Case Law Ltd (loose-leaf, bi-monthly updating service, details from Personnel Design Services, 9 Parke Road, Barnes, London SW13 9NF, tel: 01-741 3289)
● Clifton, R, *The Impact of Employment Legislation on Small Firms,* Department of Employment Research Paper No 6, 1978 (see also *Employment Gazette,* June 1978, pp 658–661 and July 1979, pp 652–655)
● Consumers Association, *Getting a New Job,* Consumers Association, London 1981
● Field, D, *Hotel and Catering Law in Britain,* 4th edition, Sweet and Maxwell, London 1982

●*5 Star News,* The Hotel and Catering Workers' Union's newspaper published by HCWU (address in Appendix II)

●Fox, A, *Industrial Sociology and Industrial Relations,* Royal Commission on Trade Unions and Employers' Associations Research Paper No 3, HMSO, London 1966

●Incomes Data Services, *Catering Pay,* IDS, London 1980, IDS Study No 222 (an interesting survey of pay and conditions in the industry, it indicates that most workers are paid just above the wages council minimum and suggests that some employers will pay higher rates to keep the union out) details from IDS, address on page 110.

●Labour Research Department, *Bargaining Report* (and other occasional publications, details from Labour Research Department, 78 Blackfriars Road, London SE1 8HF, tel: 01-928 3649

●Magurn, J P, *A Manual of Staff Management in the Hotel and Catering Industry,* 4th edition, Heinemann, London 1984

●Mars, G, Mitchell, P, Bryant, D, *Manpower Problems in the Hotel and Catering Industry,* Saxon House/Gower Press, Farnborough 1978

●Mars, G, Nicoll, M, *The Secret World of Waiters – Manipulations, Manoeuvres and the Customer,* Allen and Unwin, London, 1984

●McMullen, J, *Rights at Work,* 1978 and *Employment Law under the Tories,* 1981, Pluto Press (in the series *Worker Guides to Employment Law and Practice*)

●National Council for Civil Liberties, *Your Rights at Work,* 3rd edition, 1983, details from the National Council at 21 Tabard Street, London SE1 4LA

●Richards, M, Stewart, S W, *Legal Aspects of the Hotel and Catering Industry,* 2nd edition, Bell and Hyman, London 1979

●Workers' Educational Association, *Law at the Workplace,* (an information pack) details from the Association at 9 Upper Berkeley Street, London W1H 7BY, tel: 01-402 5608/9.

Appendix IV

Checklist of employment legislation

It can be useful to be able to refer to the original document when resolving a particularly difficult problem. Acts of Parliament may initially look forbidding, but are worth consulting once you know how they are laid out – each Act contains a comprehensive list and description of contents, as well as a section entitled *Interpretation* which defines terms used in the Act.

The list below covers the relevant legislation. Copies of the Acts can be obtained from HMSO or through booksellers:

Truck Acts 1831 to 1940
Young Persons (Employment) Act 1938
Disabled Persons (Employment) Acts 1944 and 1958
Shops Act 1950
Offices, Shops and Railway Premises Act 1963
Redundancy Payments Act 1965 (now largely replaced by the Employment Protection (Consolidation) Act 1978)
Equal Pay Act 1970
Trade Union and Labour Relations Act 1974
Rehabilitation of Offenders Act 1974
Health and Safety at Work, etc, Act 1974
Employment Protection Act 1975
Sex Discrimination Act 1975
Race Relations Act 1976
Trade Union and Labour Relations (Amendment) Act 1976
Employment Protection (Consolidation) Act 1978
Wages Councils Act 1979
Employment Act 1980
Employment Act 1982
Social Security and Housing Benefits Act 1982

Appendix V

Code of practice: Disciplinary
Employment, ACAS, 1977

Employee Relations

Amendment

The statutory provisions listed below referreu ᴜᴜ ⸻
have been repealed and re-enacted as provisions of the
Employment Protection (Consolidation) Act 1978, as follows:

(a) The Contracts of Employment Act 1972 (as amended by
the Employment Protection Act 1975) has been replaced by
Section 1 of EP(C)A 1978 [paragraph 3 below and the
footnote[1]].

(b) The Trade Union and Labour Relations Act 1974
Schedule 1, paragraph 21(4), as amended by the Employment
Protection Act 1975 Schedule 16, Part III has been replaced by
Section 67(2) of EP(C)A [footnote[2]].

Introduction

This code supersedes paragraphs 130 to 133 (inclusive) of the
code of practice in effect under Part 1 of Schedule 1 to the
Trade Union and Labour Relations Act 1974, which paragraphs
shall cease to have effect on the date on which this code comes
into effect.

1 This document gives practical guidance on how to draw up
disciplinary rules and procedures and how to operate them
effectively. Its aim is to help employers and trade unions as
well as individual employees – both men and women –
wherever they are employed regardless of the size of the
organisation in which they work. In the smaller establishments
it may not be practicable to adopt all the detailed provisions,
but most of the features listed in paragraph 10 could be
adopted and incorporated into a simple procedure.

Why have disciplinary rules and procedures?

2 Disciplinary rules and procedures are necessary for
promoting fairness and order in the treatment of individuals
and in the conduct of industrial relations. They also assist an
organisation to operate effectively. Rules set standards of
conduct at work; procedure helps to ensure that the standards
are adhered to and also provides a fair method of dealing with
alleged failures to observe them.

3 It is important that employees know what standards of
conduct are expected of them and the Contracts of

115

Employment Act 1972 (as amended by the Employment Protection Act 1975) requires employers to provide written information for their employees about certain aspects of their disciplinary rules and procedures[1].

4 The importance of disciplinary rules and procedures has also been recognised by the law relating to dismissals, since the grounds for dismissal and the way in which the dismissal has been handled can be challenged before an industrial tribunal[2]. Where either of these is found by a tribunal to have been unfair the employer may be ordered to reinstate or re-engage the employees concerned and may be liable to pay compensation to them.

Formulating policy

5 Management is responsible for maintaining discipline within the organisation and for ensuring that there are adequate disciplinary rules and procedures. The initiative for establishing these will normally lie with management. However, if they are to be fully effective the rules and procedures need to be accepted as reasonable both by those who are to be covered by them and by those who operate them. Management should therefore aim to secure the involvement of employees and all levels of management when formulating new or revising existing rules and procedures. In the light of particular circumstances in different companies and industries trade union officials[3] may or may not wish to participate in the formulation of the rules but they should participate fully with management in agreeing the procedural arrangements which will apply to their members and in seeing that these arrangements are used consistently and fairly.

[1]Contracts of Employment Act 1972 S.4(2) as amended by Employment Protection Act Schedule 16 Part II requires employers to provide employees with a written statement of the main terms and conditions of their employment. Such statements must also specify any disciplinary rules applicable to them and indicate the person to whom they should apply if they are dissatisfied with any disciplinary decision. The statement should explain any further steps which exist in any procedure for dealing with disciplinary decisions or grievance. The employer may satisfy these requirements by referring the employees to a reasonably accessible document which provides the necessary information.

[2]The Trade Union and Labour Relations Act 1974 Schedule 1 paragraph 21(4), as amended by the Employment Protection Act Schedule 16 Part III specified that a complaint of unfair dismissal has to be presented to an industrial tribunal before the end of the three month period beginning with the effective date of termination.

[3]Throughout this code, 'trade union official' has the meaning assigned to it by S.30(1) of the Trade Union and Labour Relations Act 1974 and means, broadly, officers of the union, its branches and sections, and anyone else, including fellow employees, appointed or elected under the union's rules to represent members.

Rules

6 It is unlikely that any set of disciplinary rules can cover all circumstances that may arise: moreover the rules required will vary according to particular circumstances such as the type of work, working conditions and size of establishment. When drawing up rules the aim should be to specify clearly and concisely those necessary for the efficient and safe performance of work and for the maintenance of satisfactory relations within the workforce and between employees and management. Rules should not be so general, as to be meaningless.

7 Rules should be readily available and management should make every effort to ensure that employees know and understand them. This may be best achieved by giving every employee a copy of the rules and by explaining them orally. In the case of new employees this should form part of an induction programme.

8 Employees should be made aware of the likely consequences of breaking rules and in particular they should be given a clear indication of the type of conduct which may warrant summary dismissal.

Essential features of disciplinary procedures

9 Disciplinary procedures should not be viewed primarily as a means of imposing sanctions. They should also be designed to emphasise and encourage improvements in individual conduct.

10 Disciplinary procedures should:

(a) be in writing;

(b) specify to whom they apply;

(c) provide for matters to be dealt with quickly;

(d) indicate the disciplinary actions which may be taken;

(e) specify the levels of management which have the authority to take the various forms of disciplinary action, ensuring that immediate superiors do not normally have the power to dismiss without reference to senior management;

(f) provide for individuals to be informed of the complaints against them and to be given an opportunity to state their case before decisions are reached;

(g) give individuals the right to be accompanied by a trade union representative or by a fellow employee of their choice;

(h) ensure that, except for gross misconduct, no employees are dismissed for a first breach of discipline;

(i) ensure that disciplinary action is not taken until the case has been carefully investigated;

(j) ensure that individuals are given an explanation for any penalty imposed;

(k) provide a right of appeal and specify the procedure to be followed.

The procedure in operation

11 When a disciplinary matter arises, the supervisor or manager should first establish the facts promptly before recollections fade, taking into account the statements of any available witnesses. In serious cases consideration should be given to a brief period of suspension while the case is investigated and this suspension should be with pay. Before a decision is made or penalty imposed the individual should be interviewed and given the opportunity to state his or her case and should be advised of any rights under the procedure, including the right to be accompanied.

12 Often supervisors will give informal oral warnings for the purpose of improving conduct when employees commit minor infringements of the established standards of conduct. However, where the facts of a case appear to call for disciplinary action, other than summary dismissal, the following procedure should normally be observed:

(a) In the case of minor offences the individual should be given a formal oral warning or if the issue is more serious, there should be a written warning setting out the nature of the offence and the likely consequences of further offences. In either case the individual should be advised that the warning constitutes the first formal stage of the procedure.

(b) Further misconduct might warrant a final written warning which should contain a statement that any recurrence would lead to suspension or dismissal or some other penalty, as the case may be.

(c) The final step might be disciplinary transfer, or disciplinary suspension without pay (but only if these are allowed for by an express or implied condition of the contract of employment), or dismissal, according to the nature of the misconduct. Special consideration should be given before imposing disciplinary suspension without pay and it should not normally be for a prolonged period.

13 Except in the event of an oral warning, details of any disciplinary action should be given in writing to the employee and if desired, to his or her representative. At the same time the employee should be told of any rights of appeal, how to make it and to whom.

14 When determining the disciplinary action to be taken the supervisor or manager should bear in mind the need to satisfy the test of reasonableness in all the circumstances. So far as possible, account should be taken of the employee's record and any other relevant factors.

15 Special consideration should be given to the way in which disciplinary procedures are to operate in exceptional cases. For example:

(a) *Employees to whom the full procedure is not immediately available.* Special provisions may have to be made for the handling of disciplinary matters among nightshift workers, in isolated locations or depots or others who may pose particular problems for example because no one is present with the necessary authority to take disciplinary action or no trade union representative is immediately available.

(b) *Trade union officials.* Disciplinary action against a trade union official can lead to a serious dispute if it is seen as an attack on the union's functions. Although normal disciplinary standards should apply to their conduct as employees, no disciplinary action beyond an oral warning should be taken until the circumstances of the case have been discussed with a senior trade union representative or full-time official.

(c) *Criminal offences outside employment.* These should not be treated as automatic reasons for dismissal regardless of whether the offence has any relevance to the duties of the individual as an employee. The main considerations should be whether the offence is one that makes the individual unsuitable for his or her type of work or unacceptable to other employees. Employees should not be dismissed solely because a charge against them is pending or because they are absent through having been remanded in custody.

Appeals

16 Grievance procedures are sometimes used for dealing with disciplinary appeals though it is normally more appropriate to keep the two kinds of procedure separate since the disciplinary issues are in general best resolved within the organisation and need to be dealt with more speedily than others. The external stages of a grievance procedure may however, be the appropriate machinery for dealing with appeals against disciplinary action where a final decision within the organisation is contested or where the matter becomes a collective issue between management and a trade union.

17 Independent arbitration is sometimes an appropriate means of resolving disciplinary issues. Where the parties concerned agree, it may constitute the final stage of procedure.

Records

18 Records should be kept, detailing the nature of any breach of disciplinary rules, the action taken and the reasons for it, whether an appeal was lodged, its outcome and any subsequent developments. These records should be carefully safeguarded and kept confidential.

19 Except in agreed special circumstances breaches of disciplinary rules should be disregarded after a specified period of satisfactory conduct.

Further action

20 Rules and procedures should be reviewed periodically in the light of any developments in employment legislation or industrial relations practice and, if necessary, revised in order to ensure their relevance and effectiveness. Any amendments and additional rules imposing new obligations should be introduced only after reasonable notice has been given to all employees and, where appropriate, their representatives have been informed.

Acknowledgement:
ACAS Code of
Practice 1 is
reproduced with the
permission of the
Controller of Her
Majesty's Stationery
Office. It is Crown
copyright.

Appendix VI

HCITB regional and area offices

Head office and London region
PO Box 18, Ramsey House, Central Square
Wembley, Middlesex HA9 7AP
Tel: 01-902 8865

West & Wales region
West Wing, Prudential Building
Wine Street, Bristol BS1 2PH
Tel: (0272) 24074

North West region
The Graftons, Stamford New Road
Altrincham WA14 1DQ
Tel: 061-928 2761

Scottish region
10 Magdala Crescent
Edinburgh EH12 5BE
Tel: 031-337 2339

North East region
2nd Floor, Stonebow House
The Stonebow, York YO1 2NP
Tel: (0904) 26134

South & East region (southern area)
2nd Floor, Ansvar House
31 St Leonard's Road, Eastbourne BN21 3UU
Tel: (0323) 20579

South & East region (eastern area)
Old Courts, All Saints Road
Newmarket, Suffolk CB8 8HH
Tel: (0638) 664948/668037

Index

Page numbers printed in bold indicate main entries

Index

Index